D0505994

The Football League Book 1

Football League Book 1

Edited by

Harry Brown

Public Relations Officer, The Football League,
Editor of The Football League Review

Assisted by

Bob Baldwin

Deputy editor Football League Review
and **Walter Pilkington**

Unsigned Contributions by

**Eric Howarth, Norman Thomas and George Readle
of the Football League Staff**

Photographs by Football League Photographer

Peter Robinson

Arthur Barker Limited

5 Winsley Street London W1

SBN 213 00169 1

Printed in Great Britain
by C. Tinling & Co. Ltd, Prescot and London

Contents

FOOTBALL LEAGUE STAFF AS AT JULY 1st 1970

League Secretary:	ALAN HARDAKER.
Private Secretary:	MRS. BARBARA ROBINSON.
Assistant Secretary:	ERIC HOWARTH.
Secretary:	PAT CALLON.
League Accountant:	NORMAN THOMAS.
Assistant:	GRAHAM KELLY (also Joint Circulation Manager, F.L.R.)
Secretaries:	RUTH FAWCETT, ANITA PEARSON.
Referees Officer:	GEORGE READLE.
Assistant:	LEON WALKER (also Joint Circulation Manager, F.L.R.)
Secretary:	SANDRA JAKENS.
Clerk:	TINA INGHAM.
Public Relations Officer and Editor, Football League Review:	HARRY BROWN.
Assistant P.R.O. and Deputy Editor:	BOB BALDWIN.
Editorial Assistant:	WALTER PILKINGTON.
Football League Staff Photographer:	PETER ROBINSON.
Secretary:	MRS. JEAN HAINSWORTH.
Subscriptions Secretary:	MRS. ZENA BROWN.
Football League Review Sales and Advertising Manager, F.L.R.	STUART EADON.
Committee Assistant, T.V. and Referees Assessors:	MACK DUERDEN.
Office Manager:	A. H. JOHNSON.
Records Office:	MRS. JEAN KNOTT, SUSAN HARDAKER.
Shorthand Typist:	SUSAN ALLEN.
General Clerks:	PAM HILLIARD, SUSAN CLARK.

Foreword

by MR. L. T. SHIPMAN
(*President, The Football League*)

It is now 82 years since The League's foundation and this Football League book is another example of the efforts our organisation is making to keep in touch with the game's supporters.

We have learned a great deal from our expansion into the field of public and press relations. In this day and age of instant communication it is vital that The Football League and its clubs should be in close and intimate touch with the millions who take a deep and continuing interest in the activities of the country's major sport.

No matter whether it be a journalist, or a member of the public, who telephones or writes to our League Press Office they can be sure of courteous attention and a prompt reply.

Week in and week out throughout the season *Football League Review* carries the Football League message, and that of its clubs. Its job is to tell you what we are trying to do for the betterment of the game.

Our Public Relations staff do not make decisions, but they endeavour throughout the year to try and interpret those decisions for you. We want you to know – and understand – the game and its problems.

Having established our own magazine, we are now attempting to produce a permanent record of each season via an official Football League book, which we feel is a necessary adjunct to these activities.

If this book is a success then it is intended it should be a yearly publication. Already we have marketed a paperback 'Soccer Who's Who – the What, When, Where, How and Why of League Football', the aim of which is to provide a Football Fan Guide to all the relevant problems of ticket booking, ground accommodation, travel and parking problems, foreign club addresses and so on and so forth which irritate the true fan because no-one seems to have provided ready answers.

As we expand into this field of communication with the public, so shall we learn. Whatever the outcome, no-one can accuse us of not trying.

Unlucky 13 ? – Judge for yourself

ALAN HARDAKER (*Secretary, The Football League*)

It is now more than thirteen years since I was appointed Secretary of The Football League on New Year's Day 1957. In this first-ever League Book it is relevant to look back to see what has happened during my period of office.

I have been privileged to be associated with more than one major change in The League structure as well as several alterations in approach to various peripheral activities. Negotiations with the Pools Promoters' Association provided the first step into a new era.

When the copyright case on League fixtures was won, and negotiations were entered into with the Pools, the first agreement was for a number of years with a minimum guarantee of £250,000. The agreement now provides a minimum of £500,000 a year for the use of the fixtures.

It would be pertinent for me to say here that this is an agreement for the use of the fixtures as produced, and nothing more. Never have the Pools Promoters' Association tried to interfere in the administration of The League in any way. As a result there has been injected into The League funds to date the sum of approximately £3,750,000 which, indirectly, has been passed on to the clubs.

The next major change was the introduction of The Football League Cup Competition.

Although this was associated with me personally, perhaps because certain people thought that it would not be a success, I think a tribute must be paid to the late Sir Joseph Richards, and the then members of the Management Committee, who backed the competition to the hilt. It is a great pity that Sir Joseph did not live to see the success which the League Cup has enjoyed in its own right over the last few years.

The introduction of the Substitute rule was another controversial issue in British football, but it can hardly be said that The League introduced substitutes. They had been used for many years on the Continent, and to such an extent that, on a number of occasions in International matches, the games had to be stopped in order to allow referees to check the number of players on the field at any one time.

This built up a resistance to substitutes in British football, which

probably made everyone forget that substitutes had been allowed for a number of years in the Laws of the Game.

When The League suggested one substitute, therefore, hands were held up in horror in all quarters. It took an awful lot of persuasion on the part of The Football League before The Football Association approved the experiment for one season.

Indeed, they were so afraid of it that it was not allowed in the FA Cup Competition in that first season of experiment. Now it has been accepted in all British professional competitions.

The latest development on The Football League scene has been the introduction of *The Football League Review*. Again, it has been a target for criticism, particularly from the viewpoint of its cost. The Football League Management Committee said, when it started, that it would take two or three years to establish as The Football League's own magazine.

It has cost somewhere in the region of £180,000 to establish *League Review,* but many of the subsequent events could never have happened had it not been for its institution.

The Watney Invitation Cup Competition has injected £82,000 into professional football, some of which has been syphoned through The Football Association to the County Football Associations. The recent announcement by the Ford Motor Company of the inauguration of the Ford Sporting League this season could bring into football in the next few years approximately £750,000. If it is successful, it will perhaps pull in even more in the future.

The interest aroused in industry in the sponsorship of professional football is directly due to the propaganda which The Football League has been able to disseminate through *The Football League Review and it may well be that, within the next ten years, The Football League will have set a pattern for responsible sponsorship, which can do nothing but good for any sport.*

What Goes on Behind Those Doors at Clifton Drive South

You can tell who are the football fans among the holidaymakers who throng every summer to the beautiful seaside town of Lytham St Annes, little more than half-a-dozen miles from Blackpool on the Fylde coast in Lancashire.

They are easy to spot as they walk along the wide and spacious Clifton Drive South 100 yards or so from the town centre and little more than that from the sea.

Easy to spot . . . because they stop and stare at a detached building in its own grounds, tucked in between private hotels, luxury flats and private residences. They stare, obviously perplexed, at the front entrance over which there is a semi-circular canopy inscribed in large blue lettering:

THE FOOTBALL LEAGUE

If you are close enough you can hear them asking each other: 'What does that mean? Is it an office, or what?'

The answer is that it most certainly **is** an office. The building is the administrative headquarters of The Football League, housing a staff of nearly 30 people under the direction of League Secretary Mr Alan Hardaker.

The Football League you see, is more than the star professional players who draw in 35 million people a year to top class football in England, it is more than the 92 clubs, it is more than 92 football stadia, most of whose names are renowned throughout the land.

The Football League is the most powerful group of professional

Morning conference in the Press office. P.R.O. Harry Brown (right) with assistant Bob Baldwin list the next Football League Review content with secretary Jean Hainsworth. Also in picture is Subscriptions Secretary Zena Brown.

football clubs in the world, the oldest and strongest Football League in the world, playing the best club football in depth in the world, and attracting the largest aggregate attendances anywhere in the world.

The growth of professional football during the last decade into one of the most virile and important offshoots of the entertainment business has been no accident. Throughout the years the administrators - both amateur and professional - while rarely moving quickly enough for their detractors, have ensured that the edifice continues to expand from the solid foundations laid by its founders.

The men who founded The League in 1888 dug the foundations carefully and well . . . they established an administrative strength which exists to this day. If an organisation is to be run well, it needs the staff to keep the machine flowing smoothly, for although The Football League operates under the jurisdiction, and within the framework of, The Football Association governing body, it is completely autonomous within itself.

It makes its own decisions, is master of its own destinies, has powerful voices within the counsels of The Football Association because within its orbit are the most powerful and influential clubs in the country, from whose supporters flows the vast majority of the cash which keeps the game, both amateur and professional, senior as well as junior, ticking and kicking.

Each First and Second Division club is a shareholder in The Football League Limited, with its own vote, while the Third and Fourth Division clubs are Associate Members with four voting shares between them. The Clubs elect a League President, and eight members, to form a Management Committee from club directors, who direct The League and its clubs, carrying out the wishes of the Annual General Meeting.

It is not the intention, or the function, here to describe the various

The large Records office and Filing Department where minute books, agendas, gate returns, handbooks, correspondence and all the impediments of administration are stored.

responsibilities and duties of the President and his Committee, or to explain the time they devote, not only to their own and to FA Committees, but to international and other counsels. Let us tell you about the Headquarters office and what makes it tick . . . to explain who works there, and what they do.

Supervising the work of the office is The League Secretary, Alan Hardaker, the professional advisor to The League, its Management Committee and its clubs. His function is to ensure that the advice the Committee receives is wise counsel like that which led The League to decide on substitutes when others were against them, which introduced the highly successful League Cup competition, when even many of the clubs themselves could see no purpose in it.

The Secretary's responsibilities to the professional game are heavy, his influence resounding. He works closely with the League President, Mr L. T. Shipman, and his Management Committee. His is the Aunt Sally job in the game, but a job which can bring many satisfactions to compensate the multitude of frustrations.

In addition to the work which he has to pursue away from the office, on other Continents and in many countries during any twelve-month period, he also supervises this Headquarters of close on thirty people who help to administer The Football League under his guidance.

What goes on at Headquarters? Head Office routine. Every player

The Football League Secretary's weekly conference with his senior staff. *Left to right:* Alan Hardaker, Eric Haworth (assistant secretary, The Football League), Norman Thomas (accountant), Harry Brown (Press Officer) and George Readle (referees).

with a League club has to sign forms and documents of registration as a Football League player; copies of every contract are lodged in the office along with the registration forms, each one of which has to be scrutinised to ensure its contents are within the Regulations.

The files reveal the personal football history of every player who ever signed for a League club, every transfer fee paid, and that would be the subject for so many corrections in the record books, if League Rule didn't insist that all transactions are private.

In one section of the office girl clerks work on the Provident and Pension Funds for players, managers and staffs. In another section they document the financial receipts from each game and record the 4% fee which comes to The League. In yet another girls work on club reports. In the same section they tabulate players' appearances and match results; in yet another department every match for the following month is given a match referee and two linesmen. It is here that club markings on referees are assessed and rated, and where reports from the official Assessors, a panel of more than 40 former top referees, are analysed.

All day the telephone is ringing. Clubs are raising queries, placing matters in dispute for adjudication. Most of the business, the ticklish queries, the day-to-day problems end on the desk of The League Secretary or his assistant secretary, Mr Eric Howarth. The financial problems are handled by the department headed by the League account-

Girls at work despatching notices to League clubs. *Left to right:* Sandra Jakens, Susan Allen, Anita Pearson, Patricia Callon and Ruth Fawcett (back to camera).

ant Mr Norman Thomas, the refereeing business by Referee's Officer Mr George Readle and his assistants. Each day several hundred letters go in and out, almost as many 'phone calls are handled by the switchboard.

It all requires a vast filing system, housed in the Records office and Library, supervised by office manager Mr A. J. Johnson.

In the summer of 1967 another branch of the office was installed . . . the Press Office. The Football League, so often labelled by those who are on football's peripheral as a 'behind-the-times' organisation, surprised them all by founding a Public Relations Section from which the *Football League Review* emanates.

Now with its own weekly mouthpiece, through which it can inform the public via club programmes, The Football League has a platform from which to tell its own story, to give its own point of view. It is not enough to be doing a job away from the public gaze in Clifton Drive South, St Annes. This day and age demands that the public is kept informed about what goes on and why. That's why PRO Harry Brown, and his staff answer 100 or more Press queries and inquiries every day, and read hundreds of Press Cuttings a week to assess the image newspapers are giving the League and its clubs.

That is why there is a weekly Press Bulletin, sent to more than 250 newspapers here and abroad, why *Review* is now sent to nearly two dozen countries ... and why both this 'League Book' and the paperback, 'Soccer Who's Who' have both been published this year.

The League is eager to communicate with the public, to project professional football as Britain's top sporting entertainment. An improved communications system between The League and its clubs – and the public – has produced a greater mutual sympathy and understanding.

It is no coincidence, we think, that attendance figures these last two seasons were the best for many years, in spite of the critics who forecast a big slump when the bubble of England's 1966 World Cup success was finally pricked.

Club football of sparkling strength, in greater depth than any other country, backed by efficient administration and harnessed to an effective public relations and Information Service at League and club level, has played a dominating role in this resurgence.

In this limited space we may not have been able to capture for you the hustle and bustle of the place which is the administrative Headquarters of professional football in this country. But you'll surely be aware now that this place with the name 'The Football League' over the front entrance is a busy hive of industry day in and day out.

Without this office, or some other like it, functioning efficiently and effectively, your weekly football wouldn't be the orderly, scheduled and highly organised entertainment it is.

It is no accident that matches begin at the advertised time, that referees and linesmen – and both teams – are always there. It is no coincidence that clubs live and work together, if not always in complete harmony ... that the strict code of conduct, the Regulations, are but rarely seriously abused. It is no coincidence that professional football today is a well paid, respected occupation.

Around everything is the strength of The Football League, no matter what its cynical critics might like you to believe.

1969-70 Greatest Ever Season

'This has been the greatest season for British soccer that I can recall. General interest in the game seems to grow wider and wider, and rightly so. I have never seen so many good club matches in one season. The standard of play is improving so rapidly that it seems to be taking place momentarily before our eyes.'– DANNY BLANCHFLOWER,
Sunday Express, April 19, 1970.

BOB BALDWIN

The 71st season of League football was dominated by one single, significant feature – England's defence of the World Cup trophy in Mexico. Before a ball had been kicked in the 1969–70 campaign everyone was made aware of the tight schedule, and the importance of keeping abreast of a fixture list compiled with Mexico in mind. The clubs had to sacrifice players, time and money to fit into the England scheme of things.

The season was notable for the emergence, at last, of Everton, the return to power of such sides as Huddersfield Town and Blackpool, the further progress of The League Cup competition and the initial experiment with sponsorship – a potential lifeline for the less wealthy clubs.

Success in Europe was a keystone, with Glasgow Celtic losing the European Cup to Feyenoord of Rotterdam after beating Leeds United in the semi-finals. But Manchester City won the European Cup Winners' Cup and Arsenal revived memories of their great days by taking the Fairs Cup.

On the debit side was the sad decline of clubs of the stature of Sunderland, Sheffield Wednesday, Aston Villa and Preston North End.

Here is a resume of what happened between August 1969 and April 1970 and a reminder of the names and items which made the headlines.

August – A week before The League programme began a national newspaper reported that one and a half million pounds had been spent on the close season transfer market. Leeds United won the Charity Shield, beating Manchester City 2 – 1 at Elland Road and Allan Clarke, Leeds' expensive signing from Leicester made his debut and had 'moments of genius' according to one critic.

CHELSEA FC
Back row, left to right: Hinton, Hutchinson, Webb, Hughes, Bonetti, Dempsey, McCreadie, Hollins. *Front Row:* Birchenall, Cooke, Hinton, Boyle, Harris, Houseman, Osgood, Baldwin, Tambling.

A few days later Leeds had a preview of an important fixture later in the season when they played Celtic in a 'friendly' watched by a 65,000 crowd at Parkhead. The game ended in a 1 – 1 draw.

Everton began their season as they meant to continue with an away win at Arsenal, Crystal Palace held Manchester United to a 2 – 2 draw in their first-ever Division One game. Don Revie peeped into his crystal ball and announced that Everton were Leeds' biggest rivals and Gordon West, the Everton goalkeeper, ruled himself out of possible World Cup selection.

After a disastrous opening to the season, Manchester United dropped Bobby Charlton for a game at Goodison Park, lost 3 – 0, and then signed Ian Ure from Arsenal to strengthen their sagging defence.

Another player on the move was the much-travelled Tony Hateley who joined Birmingham City from Coventry. The season's first League tables showed Merseyside heading the First Division – Everton first then Liverpool, and Queen's Park Rangers and Sheffield United setting the pace in Division Two.

September opened with a surprise decision by Wolves' talented forward Peter Knowles. 'I cannot be a clogger and a Christian,' he decided and left football to concentrate on his work for the Jehovah's Witnesses organisation. Sir Alf Ramsey hinted that an 18-year-old playing his first season could be in the World Cup squad but revealed no names, and Sunderland had a taste of the tribulations to come, losing 2 – 1 at home

ARSENAL FC
Left to right: Rice, Sammels, Graham, Neill, Radford, George, Simpson, Barnett, Roberts, Gould, Robertson, Storey, Court, McNab, Armstrong.

to Third Division Bradford City in a League Cup Tie. In Europe Leeds scored 10 goals against Lyn Oslo of Norway at Elland Road, Liverpool completed a 14 – 0 aggregate routing of Irish part-timers Dundalk in the Fairs Cup and Ireland's chances of competing in Mexico slumped with a 0 – 0 draw against Russia in Belfast.

There were some important statements from soccer's administrators. The FA outlined new disciplinary measures in an attempt to curb a rising 'crime wave', there was news of a new pension plan for professionals by The League and a major brewery, Watney Mann, revealed plans to put £82,000 into a sponsored competition. 'The game is passing through a period of industrial revolution and I think that within the next 10 years sponsorship will spread,' said League Secretary Alan Hardaker.

October – Leeds defeated Lyon Oslo 6 – 0 in Norway to complete a 16 – 0 aggregate win, but then bowed out of The League Cup, beaten 2 – 0 in a replay by Chelsea. Referee Keith Walker featured for the second successive week in the headlines after sending off Wolves' Derek Dougan and booking two Everton players. The previous week he had allowed his watch to tick on for time wasting in the West Brom – Liverpool game. Two Fourth Division players were suspended for eight weeks each by the Football Association, and yet another referee made headlines when Kevin Howley threatened to turn the crowd out of the ground after disturbances during the Carlisle – Chelsea League Cup match. The month ended with the dismissals of Ireland, Scotland and Wales from the World Cup. Ireland were beaten 2 – 0 in Moscow, Scotland went down unluckily 3 – 2 to West Germany in Hamburg and Wales lost 3 – 1 to East Germany at Ninian Park.

November – England made their first appearance in the World Cup season and were not very impressive in beating Holland 1 – 0 in Amsterdam. The League announced that referees were to visit dressing rooms for pre-match talks with players and that notices on 'conduct and control' would be posted up in dressing rooms. At the half way stage of the season Everton held a four-point lead over Leeds at the top of the First Division. The month ended on a cold note, snow and frozen grounds causing 20 postponements and the critics began to look anxiously at that tight fixture schedule.

December – West Bromwich Albion reached Wembley by beating Carlisle United 4 – 2 on aggregate in their League Cup semi-final and a few weeks later they were joined by Manchester City who accounted for Manchester United 4 – 3 on aggregate. England gave another poor display in beating Portugal 1 – 0 at Wembley. Everton, showing signs of slipping in the Championship race, signed England full back Keith Newton from Blackburn, and another England stalwart Roger Hunt left Liverpool for Bolton. Aston Villa's board passed a vote of confidence in manager Tommy Docherty and the year ended with the news that The League and The Scottish League had formulated plans for a British Isles club competition.

January – A new decade opened with Leeds' manager Don Revie receiving the O.B.E. in the New Year's Honours List and Arsenal pipping Tottenham for the expensive signature of Peter Marinello from Hibernian. Manchester United's George Best began a 28 days' suspension period and in the Third Round of the FA Cup Swansea scored first at Leeds before losing 2 – 1. Alan Ball joined Best on the sidelines, suspended for five weeks, and when the draw for the World Cup was made in Mexico, England found themselves in the strongest group. England disappointed 75,000 Wembley fans in a goalless draw against Holland at Wembley. Tommy Docherty was dismissed as manager of

ORIENT FC
Back row, left to right: Brisley, Allen, Plume, Jones, Scrimshaw. *Middle row:* Mancini, Bowtell, Goddard, Harper, Brabrook. *Front row:* Lazarus, Bullock, Parmenter, Dyson, Rofe, Fairbrother.

Aston Villa and in the Fourth Round of the FA Cup Leeds beat amateurs Sutton 6 – 0 and United overcame City in the Manchester derby tie.

February – Derby County, enjoying tremendous success on their return to the First Division found themselves faced with possible relegation for administrative irregularities. Terry Hennessy joined the club from Nottingham Forest. George Best marked his return to the game after suspension by scoring six goals for Manchester United in an 8 – 2 FA Cup win at Northampton and later in the month Watford ended Liverpool's hopes of further Cup progress. England finally won praise for their display in Belgium with a 3 – 1 victory in which Chelsea's Peter Osgood won his first cap.

March – England's Under 23 game against Scotland at Sunderland ended in a blizzard and was abandoned after an hour with England leading 3 – 1. Leeds virtually booked their European Cup semi-final place with a 1 – 0 victory over Standard Liege in Belgium and in a League Cup Final full of good football despite a heavy Wembley pitch, Manchester City recovered after conceding an early goal to beat West Bromwich 2 – 1 after extra time. Chelsea reached the FA Cup Final beating gallant Watford 5 – 1 at Tottenham, but Manchester United and Leeds drew 0 – 0 at Hillsborough and needed two more matches before Billy Bremner scored the goal that took Leeds to Wembley. The Scottish International was also selected Footballer of the Year by the Football Writers' Association.

Internationals Martin Peters (West Ham) and Jimmy Greaves (Tottenham) swopped clubs in a beat-the-transfer deadline move, and two managers Billy Bingham (Plymouth) and Birmingham's Stan Cullis left their clubs. Sir Alf Ramsey named his squad of 28 players for Mexico, and included Nobby Stiles. The month ended with Leeds fielding an entire reserve side at Derby and losing 4 – 1.

April – Everton clinched The League Championship on a night their only challengers Leeds were losing 0 – 1 to Celtic in the European Cup semi-final at Elland Road. A day later Paul Reaney ruled himself out of the FA Cup Final and the World Cup when he broke a leg at West Ham. His Leeds' team mate Paul Madeley was named as a replacement and then opted out. Derby County were fined £10,000 and banned from Europe for a season by a joint FA–League commission. Third Division Rotherham fans got into Europe, winning a place at the European Cup Final as winners of the Kop Choir competition.

The Ford Motor Company announced details of a £100,000 Sporting

League based on goals and good behaviour on the field. The FA Cup Final between Leeds and Chelsea ended in stalemate after extra time and meant the first replay for a final since 1912. Celtic clinched their place in the European Cup Final beating Leeds 2 – 1 at Hampden Park while Manchester City and Arsenal reached the finals of the European Cup Winners' and Fairs Cups. The Home International Championship began with Wales holding England to a draw in Cardiff and Scotland beating Ireland in Belfast. Three days later Bobby Charlton won his 100th International cap and scored England's third goal in a 3 – 1 defeat of Ireland, but the tournament ended with England, Scotland and Wales joint top when England held out to a somewhat fortunate goalless draw at Hampden Park and Wales beat Ireland 1 – 0.

In a hectic climax to the season, Arsenal maintained The Football League's domination of the Fairs Cup by beating Anderlecht 4 – 3 on aggregate in the final and a day later Manchester City clinched the European Cup Winners' Cup with a 2 – 1 win over Gornik of Poland in Vienna. Chelsea hit back from behind to win the FA Cup for the first time, beating Leeds 2 – 1 after extra time in the replay at Old Trafford.

Everton are great Champions!

HARRY BROWN

It was a bitterly cold night at Goodison Park when Everton finally clinched the 71st Football League championship with a two-nil win over West Bromwich Albion last April.

The partisan Liverpool thousands bayed their welcome to the new Knights of English football, while the many neutral observers wondered just where Harry Catterick's squad stood among the all-time greats.

There were those that night, and will be now, whose memories reach back to the halcyon pre-way days, when football was played 'by ear', who will dispute the claim that they are one of the best teams ever to have won the League crown. There were those that night, and will be now, who pointed to some of the great names of post-war years like the Wolves of the late forties and the pre-Munich Manchester United, the Tottenham double-winning team . . . or even the Manchester United of European Cup-winning fame and the Leeds United of last year and the year before.

EVERTON
Everton players and officials celebrate in their dressing-room with champagne after clinching the title with a 2 – nil win over West Bromwich Albion.

Arguments will for ever rage, and individual preference must intrude with the passage of time because nothing remains static and memory plays tricks.

Yet the facts are that, in an era when collective team responsibility within a predominantly defensive framework has produced a totally different game from the one on which we of a more mature age were weaned, this Everton squad has bridged a gap between several footballing worlds.

Highly organised, running as hard and as far as any of the squads which lean so heavily on the contemporary text-books, Everton have surely shown there is still a place for the ball manipulator within the overall tactical team demands.

Only the naive would accept that Everton disdain the functional, or that they scorn the physical, in a League where the strength in depth of the opposition, the sheer weight of fixtures and the bewildering variety of playing surface conditions, demand both the functional and physical extras over the full course.

Of course they can't afford to ignore the physical demands, or the assets of organisation, imposed on them by the speed and cohesion and application in the modern game, but it is never allowed to become a predominant factor.

They prefer to play the ball about, to make space and use space, to rely on ball skills – to rely on the construction of positive situations rather than comatose the talents of others by negative checking.

In this tremendously strong First Division of ours they cannot always manage it, but oh! how they try, and as with each succeeding season the challenge at the top becomes increasingly onerous so could it also be argued that each new championship team has grangerized the extent and dimensions of the canvas of talent, ability and ambition necessary to annex the crown.

Using that approach to my orthometry I find it difficult not to assess the 1970 Everton very high on the tide-chart of time, while the youthful tinge of the squad suggests the output ratio has still to find its apex.

I like them best of all, perhaps, because Everton – you might say – are extroverts in a football world which suddenly appeared to be peopled mainly by introverts. Their heavy reliance on the arts and crafts surely legitimises the claim.

It may sound corny, but Catterick's squad reminds me of the teams I saw in my boyhood during the thirties. Of course there are clinical, functional, physical differences. Nevertheless, they remind me.

I am not one of those who yearns for the outdated stuff of pre-war, who allows a nostalgia for Alex James and Hughie Gallagher and Dixie Dean and the rest to colour my realisation that times have changed. I feel for them as I feel for my memory of the Model T Ford I envied as a schoolboy.

No, I find that the pace of thought and movement – the very concept – of the modern game both interesting and fascinating.

The defensive overtones of recent years have never subdued the appeals of the game for me to the limits of insouciance. I am never bored by football, anyway, and I believe the vast majority of followers find that even blanket defence – the Cattenacio of the Italians – has an intrinsic appeal that has, as its basis, the universal attraction of a ball game which induces a metamorphosis into the lives of those masses to whom the glamour of the football field provides the omniscient quality of spirituality which the materialistic modern way of life tends to reject. For so many football is the religion, the god-idol, if such an analogy may be forgiven.

EVERTON
Back row, left to right: Rankin, West, Barnett (now Arsenal). *Middle row:* Harry Catterick (manager), Kendall, Brown, Kenyon, Labone, Royle, Hurst, Wilf Dixon (trainer). *Front row:* Harvey, Ball, Wright, Jackson, Husband, Humphreys, Morrissey, Whittle.

I do not classify myself within this sort of collocation and yet football remains, for me, a compelling prediliction despite my involvement on the periphery of it.

The experts assure us that defensive extremes can only get worse before the footballing scene gets better, more adventurous. And who am I to argue with experts?

But teams like Everton do most strongly suggest that even within the restrictions of the contemporary scene it is not always essential to conform, to slavishly copy, to reach out for success; it can still find its own level.

They suggest that football can still be adventurous, and exciting, as well as fascinating and interesting.

Now they have won through to success, Everton will be copied, too. I'm glad of it. Aren't you?

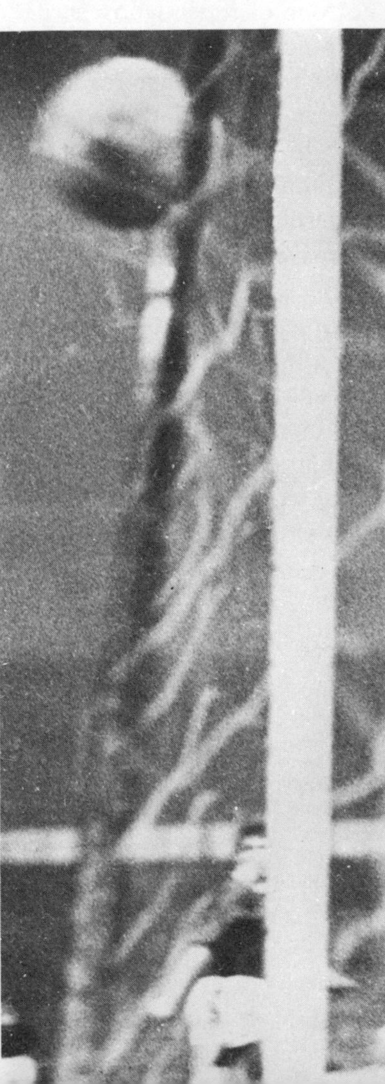

Everton needed two points from their home game against West Bromwich Albion on April 1st to make certain of the League Championship. They began nervously on a heavy pitch but when they settled down the young Albion, including four teenagers, were never in the hunt. Harvey scored one of the goals that gave Everton victory. He picked up a ball from Morrissey on the edge of the box, threaded this way and that past four defenders and hit a right foot shot which Osborne didn't even see. A goal worthy of the occasion.

What Took Everton Out of the Rut

RAY MINSHULL

What took Everton out of the rut last season to their convincing championship success? Was there any special feature of the team which shook them out of the pack into the front-running position?

The Football Association's North West Regional coach, Ray Minshull, *says there was. In this article he points to the Goodison 'Engine Room' and suggests that this was the key to Everton's Championship success.*

The names of Alan Ball, Howard Kendall and Colin Harvey represent one of the most talented midfield trios in The Football League. Evertonians are proud of their 'Engine Room'.

any team. It is not just a question of winning the ball but, having gained possession, knowing the most successful way to use it. The Everton midfield trio are adept at both.

The abundance of talent displayed by these three accomplished players is well known, but each has a particular role to play both individually and collectively. Howard Kendall is a long-striding player who is always at his best when going forward to accept the ball played into spaces created by his colleagues. On many occasions these excursions have resulted in spectacular goal-scoring efforts. While Kendall is operating on these forward runs it becomes the responsibility of Harvey to move into a more central position on the field to cover any possible breakdown and threat to their defensive organisation.

Colin Harvey, the more conventional ball player, prefers the ball played to his feet when he can display his outstanding control to create positions from which he produces defence-splitting passes. When possession of the ball is lost he can always be relied upon to recover his position with a well-timed tackle, or to delay the opposition until the rest of the defence is in a covering position.

Like Kendall he is ever ready to support the attack, and go forward to create scoring opportunities. When he does, the cover in midfield becomes the responsibility of Kendall. Alan Ball is a prodigious worker, a human dynamo who demands high performance not only of himself but of all his team-mates. His acceptance of responsibility, even though things may be going badly, shows a man of courage and determination to succeed. He is a most dedicated professional and his ability not only to create, but also to take goal scoring opportunities, makes him a constant threat to any opposition.

That Everton scored more goals than any other team but Leeds in the First Division of the Football League last season, after being the top scorers the season before, must be in no small way attributed to the high standard of performance by these midfield players.

All three have played in representative games. Alan Ball, a regular member of the England squad, Colin Harvey, in the opinion of many good judges one of the finest midfield players in the country and a Mexico certainty but for his eye complaint, and Howard Kendall, an Under-23 International with every reason to anticipate many further honours in the not-too-distant future.

They are all young, experienced and accomplished players.

Team of all Talents

MATT GILLIES

(*Manager, Nottingham Forest F.C.*)

The break-through of Everton to The League Championship is a great thing for English League football simply because they have done so on the basis of footballing skills.

Success is always emulated, and if more teams try to play it the way Everton are doing then we can look forward to a more positive approach as well as more exhilarating football.

It is inevitable they will be copied. In any club the reserves and the youngsters will always emulate the senior squad, and this will now spread to other clubs just as everyone borrowed the England tactical plan which led to the 1966 World Cup success.

Everton last season were a smooth side, almost a pure footballing side. I deliberately use the word 'almost' because if you label a side as complete purists you are in fact damning them a bit, because this is the hardest and best League in the world and no-one can hope to win it without mixing in a bit of the physical.

The greatest achievement of Harry Catterick's side is that they have resorted to only the absolute minimum of physical application, and have injected the maximum possible offering of the delightful and sheer skills which make our game so attractive when played in this way.

What They Lack in Physique

DAVE SEXTON* (*Manager, Chelsea F.C.*).

It is especially satisfying to me to be able to congratulate Everton on their break-through to The League Championship in 1970 because they have exploited all the facets of the football game in which I have personally been – and always will be, I hope – a great believer.

For the last few seasons Harry Catterick's club have been so close to breaking through time and again, and it is fitting that they should have done so when English football is in the ascendancy throughout Europe

* In an interview with Bob Baldwin.

and making such a world impact despite what may or may not happen in Mexico after this is written.

Perhaps Everton's greatest triumph is that their achievement has been attained with a set of small players up front, with the exception of Joe Royle. Because of this lack of size and weight they have leaned heavily on midfield crafts supplied in crisp and snappy fashion by Alan Ball, Colin Harvey and Howard Kendall.

That is where their real strength lies, and we can expect them to develop further with lads like Alan Whittle and Joe Royle increasing even further the sharpness in front of goal.

Now they are on top be sure they will take a lot of knocking off.

Second Division Champions – Huddersfield Town

BOB BALDWIN

When Huddersfield Town climbed to the top of the Second Division in the early weeks of last season, the more hardened supporters in the Yorkshire town were not impressed. They had seen it all before.

'Wait until Christmas,' the cynics cried, remembering previous bright starts to seasons and a gradual decline around the turn of each year.

So when Huddersfield kept up their promotion challenge throughout Christmas with a home win over strong-running Sheffield United and a win at Bristol City, even teetotal Manager, Ian Greaves, allowed himself a glass of sherry. From then on Town were never off the top and cantered back into the First Division after fourteen seasons out of it.

Manager Greaves told me, 'Looking back, Christmas was the make-or-break period. Some of our supporters had come to expect our falling away then after a good start. They doubted whether we could keep it up. This was the crucial period, and when we survived it a new confidence flowed in. You could say Santa Claus definitely called in on us last year'. The Town side, average age only 21, came through with flying colours.

Ian Greaves, a former Busby Babe at Old Trafford talks proudly about his young champions. Coach at Leeds Road before taking over the Manager's reigns, he readily emphasises the relationship that has developed between everyone connected with the club, 'from the Chairman and Board downwards'.

Of his young, still-learning side that carried the club back into soccer's top flight Greaves says: 'Four or five of them joined the club from school while I was coach. I knew them, they knew me as a hard man but a fair one. We started on the right lines the season before last when we finished sixth in the Second Division, and last season we continued from where we left off.'

HUDDERSFIELD TOWN
Back row, left to right: Ian Greaves (Manager), Dick Krzywicki, Terry Poole, Roy Ellam, Brian Greenhalgh, Trevor Cherry, Dennis Clarke, David Lawson, Ray Mielczarek, Colin Dobson, Henry Cockburn (Chief Coach). *Front row:* Steve Smith, Jimmy Lawson, Les Chapman, Jimmy McGill, Frank Worthington, Bobby Hoy, Geoff Hutt, Jimmy Nicholson.
*Picture copyright of the Huddersfield Examiner.

The Huddersfield Manager lays special emphasis on the work off the field at Leeds Road. 'I know the game is won or lost in 90 minutes on the field,' he says, 'but football penetrates psychologically deeper than that. One of the reasons for our promotion was the building of a players' lounge and the development of the club offices. Some of the players' wives, living on different sides of the town, did not know each other until then. Spirit on the field is developed off the pitch, and we clinched it with that piece of enterprise'.

The one blemish in an otherwise outstanding season, as far as the Manager was concerned, was a 4 – 1 defeat at Aston Villa. The side revealed its true character by winning the next game 4 – 0. They are quick learners.

THIRD DIVISION CHAMPIONS
ORIENT
Manager Jimmy Bloomfield shouts instructions during a hectic training session at Brisbane Road.

'We gained promotion by playing football in every match,' Greaves points out. 'We did not kick our way to the top. I am optimistic about our chances in the First Division because with a very young side, we can only progress. The players will mature quickly in the better class of football.'

Greaves is reluctant to pick out particular players for praise – 'it was a team effort', he emphasises. But he singles out his captain, Jimmy Nicholson. 'Not because he played better than anyone else, but because he carried the extra responsibilities of leading the side and providing the balance of experience for the youngsters around him.'

Huddersfield, once accused of living in the past, do not intend to stand still. Ian Greaves is a shining example. Only a few days after the club had clinched promotion, Greaves signed on for a close season coaching course at Lilleshall. 'You can never stop learning and picking up new ideas,' he says. 'I must progress, just like my team.'

The stiffer challenge of the new season will test Town, but of one thing I'm sure . . . every game will find them absorbing new lessons.

I for one believe Huddersfield will also learn to quickly apply them.

HUDDERSFIELD
Town manager Ian Greaves receives a gallon bottle of Bell's Scotch Whisky, and a £100 cheque, for being elected Manager of the Month last January. Making the presentation is Arthur Bells & Sons Sales Manager Anthony Derry with

Third Division Champions–Orient

Manager Jimmy Bloomfield, a skilful inside forward rated unlucky not to have got nearer an England cap than Under 23 appearances, leaned on the experience he gained playing against the crack sides of a decade ago to guide Orient back into the Second Division after four years on the sidelines.

Recruited as player-manager two years ago Bloomfield, whose playing career took him from Brentford to Arsenal, Birmingham, West Ham and Plymouth, uses one word to explain Orient's success: consistency.

'I look back on the great sides I played against – the pre-Munich Manchester United and the Spurs' double side especially, and I remember how well they functioned in all conditions. This is what we have striven for at Brisbane Road.'

It was consistency on the bone-hard pitches of early season, and on the clinging-mud surfaces of mid-winter, that kept Orient in touch with the promotion race right through the season.

The season before, Orient finished just two points higher than relegated Northampton Town. 'That season was nowhere near a true reflection of our potential.'

Mark Lazarus, fresh from fighting a successful promotion battle for Crystal Palace, was recruited to add experience to a mainly home-grown line up. Barrie Fairbrother, Tommy Taylor and Denis Rofe ('the best young back anywhere in the game,' says his Manager) developed in stature as the pressures of promotion built up.

Although injuries hit the team fairly frequently, Bloomfield reflects: 'One of the most pleasing factors about the season was the way we managed to keep picking up points without senior players, absent because of injury.' Terry Mancini, lynch-pin of the defence, was missing for seven games after Christmas, five away from home. Yet Orient were never very far from the top.

Two matches stand out in Bloomfield's mind . . . matches he rates as those which clinched a place in Division Two. The first was when promotion rivals Luton Town were beaten in front of an 18,000 Boxing Day crowd at Brisbane Road, and the second was an away win at Torquay in January when Luton were going down at home to Plymouth.

Now Orient are geared to the task of making an impression on the Second Division. 'Given the breaks, I think we can hold our own,' says Jimmy Bloomfield. 'Everybody needs the breaks.'

Fourth Division Champions–Chesterfield

Back in the days when Queen Victoria proudly sat on the throne of Empire, early pioneers were developing the game of soccer in the North Derbyshire town of Chesterfield.

The records show that the town, famous for its crooked spire, played football as long ago as 1866 and boasted a organised club in 1871.

So it was appropriate that the modern footballers of Chesterfield should celebrate the anniversary in style a year early by winning the Fourth Division championship.

Even then, some people claimed, Chesterfield were two years late. The club were poised for promotion, only to falter in the vital final weeks of the 1967–8 season. The following season they struggled and avoided the bottom four by only two points. From that near-disastrous campaign came the blueprint from which promotion was drawn up – Chesterfield's youngsters last year won the Intermediate Cup against reserve sides from clubs with far greater all-round resources.

CHESTERFIELD
Left to right: Hickton, Archer, Moore, Holmes, Carline, Pugh, Martin, Walker, Moyes, Randall, Lumsden, Fenoughty, Humphreys, Phelan, Wright, Stevenson, Moss and Bell.

'Success in that competition showed we had the potential within the club,' says manager Jimmy McGuigan. 'We were able to build on this, and with the addition of two experienced players in Tom Fenoughty from Sheffield United and John Archer from Huddersfield, we gathered a squad of 15 or 16 players which I thought would do well.'

On reflection Jimmy McGuigan feels that missing promotion two seasons ago was a real boon. 'We were not really ready,' he points out, 'and would have struggled to have stayed up. We were given the chance to start again, and by concentrating on youth we have players who are ambitious enough to face the challenge of football in a higher grade.'

The club have training facilities at Eckington, near Saltergate, to match any in the lower divisions. 'We use it every day of the week,' says McGuigan, 'and endeavour to make the best of what we have.'

The club also hold their own in the fiercely competitive business of discovering and signing young players in the region. 'I lay special emphasis on this, and count myself fortunate in having a chief scout like Reg Wright who has spent all his life developing youngsters in the area.'

Twenty years ago Chesterfield were proud members of the Second Division. No-one at the Saltergate Ground is naive enough to prophesy a sudden return to these pastures, but the club's success last season has prompted optimism in Chesterfield that a return to 'the good old days' may be just around the corner.

The 1969–70 Team That Nobody Could ignore—Leeds United

HARRY BROWN

Perhaps Leeds United's finest moment last season came off the field of play ... the night after their European Cup semi-final exit at the hands of Glasgow Celtic at Hampden Park in mid April.

Manager Don Revie told a nation-wide audience on BBC television: 'Wę were twice beaten by a better team. Celtic were magnificent.'

Not one excuse. Not one complaint.

There were those of us who would have pointed to the season curtailed because of World Cup demands, to the tremendous strains imposed upon the Leeds squad by the chase for the triple crowns of The League championship and the European and F A Cups . . . to the extra burdens imposed by a catastrophic run of injuries . . . to the fixture pile-up. Revie uttered none of these in public, and thereby grew in stature.

Leeds United, acknowledged by all well into the year as the most complete squad in English football – albeit a grudging acknowledgement by some – finally won nothing at all. It was both a shock to most of the rest of us, and a terrible anti-climax for the club.

The rigours of a desperately testing season had finally beaten Leeds, but the skill of every member of the squad remained unquestioned.

Nevertheless they enter the 1970–71 season with a question mark hanging like a shroud across their shoulders: will the long-term effect of last season leave them stranded mentally and physically below the high-water mark of ambition, or will it galvanise their determination towards new plateaux of achievement? Only time will tell.

No-one who saw them against Chelsea at Wembley could fail to have been impressed by their accurate, immaculate football or their compressed efficiency. It was a game they should have won, but didn't. The Fates by then had stopped smiling, Lady Luck had gone sour. It curdled completely in the replay. They failed to improve on a lone Jones goal, despite all the run of the game and were taken into extra time to lose finally 2 – 1. It was as though they were destined to win nothing.

Don Revie in one newspaper interview attributed the late season slump to the demands of three targets in a tightly compressed season and to the loss, just before Wembley, of Paul Reaney. There is no justification for querying this assessment.

The fact remains that Leeds United, dubbed by many as too clinical and too physical in 1967–8, when they also finished as perennial bridesmaids, produced attacking overtones and positive, constructive football in the Championship year of 1968–9 which flowered last season into a forceful panoramic of all that is best in the British game until events so cruelly overtook the Elland Road squad.

The backroom staff realise only too well that a team has got to keep on the move, has got to keep on improving and to be improved – and that one season's disappointments must somehow provide the impetus for the following season's assault. Unless the impetus is maintained then there is only one other way to go.

At this stage in an era, which began with Don Revie finding the club poised on the brink of Division Three, one can only imagine that to be unthinkable.

Support, The Basis of the Leeds United Game

JOHN ADAMS (*FA Regional Coach, North of England*)

From the time Association Football was first played one facet of it has always been fundamental to success, the one described as 'Support'.

Soccer is a team game. The most brilliant individual player is unable completely to control the course of events. The higher the level of his individual ability, the longer he may be able to keep the ball and prevent

LEEDS UNITED
Back row, left to right: Clarke, Sprake, Harvey, Hunter, Charlton. *Middle row:* Yorath, Gray, Belfitt, Madeley, Jones, Lorimer. *Front row:* Bates, Giles, Cooper, Bremner, Hibbitt.

the opposition from using it, but ultimately he will require aid from his colleagues, either in attack or defence, and this can be classified as 'Support'.

Generalisations are always dangerous, but one could certainly point to an understanding of 'Support' in attack and defence as being a tremendous factor in the success story of Leeds United.

In attack – that is to say when they have the ball – Leeds are constantly and quickly providing passing alternatives for the player on the ball. Obviously speed in providing close support for a player with the ball under pressure is essential if ball possession is to be retained, but if penetration is to be achieved it is important that players in more advanced positions seek to make runs into areas where the ball can be played to them. Leeds invariably manage to succeed in difficult circumstances. Their players all run to attain support positions when the ball is being played, and for the next ball when this is achieved.

Often the ball is played out long from Normal Hunter or Jack Charlton to Mick Jones, who is really acting as a target man. Even while the ball is on its way Billy Bremner and Johnny Giles, or Mick Bates, will be covering ground to provide the essential possession-retaining support positions. At the same time Allan Clarke, Peter Lorimer or even Eddie Gray will be engaged in making runs designed to take them into advance positions round the back of defenders so that the ball can be played to them to complete the attack.

Where 'Support' is non-existent, or bad support angles developed, this effectiveness is made less, and consequently unless the individual receiving the ball has the highest individual skill, the possibilities of the attack continuing successfully is slight. Obviously therefore 'Support' in attack is essential as it is in defence.

'Support' is fundamental to their thinking in terms of defence. Defence begins when possession of the ball is lost, wherever on the pitch that may be, and more and more players are being required to know how to defend. This, of course, includes 'Forwards' – that is to say those usually wearing shirts No's 7 to 11 – as well as the more traditional defenders.

The object of much of this defence initially is to cut down the opposition's passing angles by putting pressure on the man with the ball. Defending from the front is a feature of the play of Leeds and Mick Jones must surely rank as one of the best 'defenders' in the ranks of British forwards.

But this good work can be minimised if the situation is allowed to remain 1 *v.* 1 (Player on ball *v.* Jones), since the player in possession may be able to dribble round, or pass the ball off.

Consequently the objects of other players on the defensive side is to cut down these possibilities. The major consideration is to prevent the attacker proceeding with the ball, and this can be effected by the development of proper support. Obviously the requirement is to get a defending player in a position close enough to his colleague to be able to 'sweep' the ball up if it is played past him.

In the Leeds context one can see this developed all the way down the line, from forwards such as Mick Jones, to basic defenders like Paul Reaney and Terry Cooper. Thus, 'Support' in defence provides the opportunity for restricting space and time available to the attacking side, and invites them to put their possession of the ball at risk if they wish to progress.

And this is what the Leeds style of play is all about.

Chelsea–Challengers in Europe

Chelsea's re-emergence last season as the South's leading challengers for honours was a triumph for all that is good in football. While never revealing the clinical proficiency of Leeds nor the overall consistency of Everton, Chelsea bred their own inimitable brand of free expressive soccer – and it carried them back into Europe.

Under the quiet but firm guiding hand of Dave Sexton, the Stamford Bridge side developed as the season progressed so that by April they were generally considered one of the most attractive sides to watch, even by those discerning followers living either side of the Pennines, although their FA Cup win over Leeds was powered by resilience rather than flair.

While Arsenal, London's leading challengers to the North in season 1968–9, relied to a large degree on a more disciplined approach to reach Europe, Chelsea combined strength at the back with a flowing, quick-break style of moving forward.

Much of their success in this direction was due to the phenomenal progress of Hudson and Hutchinson. Virtually unknown outside the immediate confines of S.W.6 in the early months of the season, the pair developed into players of immense stature and supreme potential.

Peter Houseman (left) and David Webb (right) hold the FA Cup after Chelsea had beaten Leeds United in the replay at Old Trafford. Other Chelsea players are: Tommy Baldwin (extreme left), John Dempsey (behind Baldwin) and substitute Marvin Hinton (extreme right). John Hollins is the player in the background.

They apparently lacked nothing alongside the more experienced Cooke and Osgood, and Hudson's talents in particular drew approval from even Sir Alf Ramsey. Praise indeed.

Osgood continued to reveal his unique brand of virtuosity, and despite a rather immature outburst in print when he proclaimed he would never play for England because he was too lazy, he made an impressive international debut on a gluepot of a Brussels pitch.

Alongside Chelsea's main executioners were Cooke and Houseman, the latter never quite reaping the praise Sexton's other front runners seemed to claim, yet showing against Watford in the FA Cup semi-final that he was never out of place in such austere company. Only when one remembers that waiting on the sidelines for most of the season were such players as Baldwin, Birchenhall, Boyle, Hinton, and the young Scottish goalkeeper Hughes, does one begin to grasp just how much talent Sexton has assembled at Stamford Bridge.

Behind the front runners were Hollins, never frightened to gnaw away at the opposition in midfield, the powerful defensive and overlapping qualities of McCreadie, and a pivot in Dempsey who was able to contain the very best striker.

Dempsey, Webb and the indefatigable Harris were the pillars of a defence some said was prone to crack under pressure. That it rarely showed, was due more than anything else to the supreme goalkeeping of Bonetti, back to his very best after an indifferent spell in which he was excluded from England's South American World Cup rehearsal in 1969.

Now that Chelsea seem to have rid themselves of that 'music hall' image once and for all, there seems no end to what they can achieve. Whether they can match Arsenal's sturdy re-appearance in Europe remains to be seen. One thing is for sure, if they fail it will not be through any shortage of talent.

BOB BALDWIN

After 17 years Arsenal come in From the Cold

Arsenal carried their thoughtful, disciplined game back into Europe last season and continued from where Leeds United in 1968 and Newcastle United a year later had left off, by winning The European Fairs' Cup. It was their first major trophy in 17 years.

Their successful return to Europe served to emphasise the all round strength in depth of The Football League for in domestic competitions last season, Arsenal were hardly conspicuous.

They slipped from the fourth position achieved in the First Division in 1968–9, failed to match their League Cup exploits of previous years when they reached Wembley in successive seasons, and suffered an ignominious FA Cup defeat at Blackpool.

It was a very different story when Arsenal turned their attentions to Europe. Players with the experience of McLintock, Graham and McNab plus those possessing the youthful exuberance of George thrived against Continental sides often of far greater experience in Europe.

Against the Dutch side Ajax in the semi-final Arsenal displayed tremendous maturity in virtually clinching their final place after a 3 – 0 first leg win at Highbury.

ARSENAL
John Radford – Arsenal's powerful striker with a good shot in both feet had a lot to do with his club's successful re-entry into Europe through the Fairs Cup. The honours have not deserted him either for he has been capped at under 23 and full international levels.

Many of Arsenal's League shortcomings stemmed from a mid-season injury to goalkeeper Bob Wilson who broke an arm at Burnley. Barnett, an Everton reserve with a lot of potential but little League experience, was purchased but it was obvious that Wilson's absence was badly felt in defence.

Another addition to the playing ranks was Marinello, bought for a big fee and in a glare of publicity from Hibernian. He was tagged London's George Best and in his first game for Arsenal, ironically against Manchester United at Old Trafford, he scored a goal straight from the Best text book. Unfortunately for Arsenal, Marinello took longer to adapt to the quicker pace of the English game than might have been anticipated.

The rise in stature of youngsters George, and to a lesser extent Kelly, more than compensated for loss of form by more established players at Highbury. George's explosive entry on to The League scene had some people, rather prematurely as events proved, suggesting that he could be a surprise choice for Mexico. Nevertheless, George left his mark on many defences during the season and earmarked himself as a possibility for the 1974 World Cup.

The success and experience gained in Europe will no doubt stand Arsenal in good stead in the domestic competitions to come. Having been ousted out of the Southern limelight by the accomplishments of Chelsea, Arsenal still possess the qualities needed to make a mark on the home scene over the next season or two. *BOB BALDWIN*

European Cup Winners' Cup and League Cup–What Next for Manchester City?

HARRY BROWN

A couple of years ago, when The League Championship went to Maine Road, some of the professional critics allowed themselves to extemporise their virtues before the ink was dry on the achievement.

In the event, despite their great success since in winning three Cups in just over 12 months – the FA Cup, the League Cup and the European Cup Winners' Cup in that order – Manchester City have not quite been able to justify all that eulogy.

If that sounds churlish, it is not meant to be. City have a latent beauty about their game but, too often, it remains just beneath the surface. They have not yet fulfilled all that they promise.

For the Maine Road squad have emerged as a Big Match outfit. On the big occasion all their flair, all their style, flows big; but they have too many mediocre days throughout a long League season for them yet to deserve the accolade 'great' which many critics have thrust on them.

Trace the recent history of the side which Joe Mercer and Malcolm Allison have welded together. The 1967–8 League title was won late, from behind, by a team whose football was given new impetus by the October acquisition of Francis Lee from Bolton Wanderers. It was founded on the solidity of Heslop, the drive of Book, Doyle and Oakes, the linking of Bell, and the stark striking power of Lee, Young and Summerbee.

Maybe the sudden fame and adulation thrust upon them by their unexpected League title brought the reaction of the following season. Whatever the reason their form week in and week out was unimpressive until the spectacular run which took them to Wembley. In the event they were uninspired in late April 1969 when they shakily beat relegation-haunted Leicester City by the one goal.

Manchester City captain Tony Book holds the League Cup trophy aloft after the extra-time victory against West Bromwich Albion at Wembley. The other City players are, *left to right:* Joe Corrigan, Francis Lee, George Heslop, Glyn Pardoe, Tommy Booth, Ian Bowyer and Mike Doyle.

Last season they were even more unpredictable. Some weeks they were bad – rank bad – and some weeks they were devastatingly brilliant. Rarely were they just average. A season which saw them finish half way down the Division One chart also saw them snap up two Cups in brilliant fashion.

But even in the death-or-glory League Cup they had palpitating moments, and none more so than in the two legs of the semi-finals against neighbours Manchester United which they were somewhat fortunate to win. They went to Wembley after a run of indifferent form, and were a goal down to Albion in the early minutes. They looked as though they were going to be taken to the cleaners, were pulled up by the bootlaces by Francis Lee, and proceeded to display some great football against an always mobile West Bromwich in an exciting final.

Doyle equalised in the second half and the winning goal came from Pardoe in extra time. Once again they had shown what a great side they are on the Big Occasion, and when the mood is right. In Vienna in late April they gave Gornik of Poland the run-round in the European Cup Winners' Cup Final which belied the final 2 – 1 score, and this despite problems which kept Summerbee out of the game, saw Doyle carried off early on, and had Oakes playing after a pain-killing injection.

It may sound trite to quibble about a squad which can win four major trophies in two seasons (they also pulled in the FA Charity Shield in 1968), but there can be no doubt that at Maine Road this season they will be searching for the missing link – consistency – the ability to turn it on week in and week out in all sorts of conditions and situations.

If they find it . . . then English fans can eagerly look forward to a new application of the outrageously skilful, to something extra within the accepted patterns of the footballing arts.

Probably season 1970–1 offers no bigger a challenge to anyone than to Manchester City.

Ian Bowyer celebrates Manchester City's League Cup winning goal scored by Glyn Pardoe against West Bromwich Albion at Wembley.

Football Has Its Own Bible

— An easy Guide to the
Regulations of the Football League Ltd.

DID YOU KNOW that the conduct of a club's supporters can lead to their expulsion from The Football League?

DID YOU KNOW that a club who fail to fulfil a League fixture are liable to a £5,000 fine *plus* whatever extra punishment The League Management Committee think necessary?

DID YOU KNOW that home clubs pay a percentage per spectator to visiting clubs in League matches . . . and that, no matter how small the attendance might be, the amount paid cannot be less than £200?

ALL THESE INSTRUCTIONS are among the 75 Regulations of The Football League Limited, the 'bible' of professional football. Every club secretary, every club manager, and every club Board of Directors who ignore the instructions, do so at their own peril. The penalties for evasion are heavy.

How often have you read that The Regulations are 'an anachronism from a by-gone age', meaning they are outdated and a left-over from days gone by?

Judge for yourself by checking this specially-prepared Guide to the Regulations.

The secretary of a Football League club has to be a versatile character – and a knowledgeable one.

He must have a comprehensive working knowledge of the Companies Act (all League clubs with the exception of Nottingham Forest, who are run by a Committee, are limited Companies), the Rules of The Football Association and the 75 Regulations of The Football League. It's no easy job. The League Regulations alone take some digesting.

You wouldn't imagine it takes 20,000 words to put on a professional Football League game? But it does, and if we look at the variety of subjects and conditions these Regulations cover you may begin to grasp just how complex an industry top-class football has become, and how thoroughly the founders of The League did their job. It must be stressed, however, that the Regulations are made - or changed - by the clubs themselves at League annual meetings. It is they who decide. The Management Committee's responsibility is to ensure that the Regulations are obeyed.

So much of the body of the present 'bible' originated in The League's early years, and though time has altered the phraseology and, indeed, the meaning out of all recognition, much of what was initiated then is still with us. Did you know, for instance, that the Regulations clearly define The League's Constitution?

They are: ... *to conduct and, in every respect control, each season a football competition to be called The League championship for each division, and at all times to safeguard the interests of the clubs in Full and Associate Membership of The League.*

Those are the objectives, but what about membership fees to clubs? There are none. Entrance fees for new clubs admitted to Division Four is £100; clubs promoted to Division Two have to pay a further £200. Apart from these there are no fees or subscriptions.

The size of The Football League is clearly defined by the Regulations of the F.A. for the Control of Leagues and Competitions which apply to *all* Leagues. The First and Second Divisions together must be no bigger than 44 clubs, all of whom are full members of The League with individual voting rights.

The League may also admit clubs to the Third and Fourth Divisions, but they do not have individual voting rights; they are only Associated Members of The League and are allowed one vote for every 11 clubs.

Collectively they have four votes between them. Votes can only be cast by club Directors or committee men, and no decision on any matter, nor one word of the Regulations, can be changed except by a three-quarters voting majority so it is readily apparent that the bigger clubs have the most powerful voices. One more vote is available, that of The President of the League - at present Mr L. T. Shipman, M.B.E.

The big decisions are usually made at the Annual General Meeting, but urgent matters which arise at other times of the year can be decided at extraordinary general meetings.

At any General Meeting, for example, a three-quarters majority could expel any club whose conduct, or the conduct of whose players or officials or supporters, is considered to warrant such drastic action.

Except at General Meetings the affairs of The League are conducted by a Management Committee consisting of a President, two vice Presidents and six members, all of whom must be club directors or committee men. Only First and Second Division representatives can be elected to the Committee, but if a member's club is relegated to the Third Division during his term of office he can put himself forward for re-election. Members of the Management Committee hold office for three years at the end of which they have to seek re-election at the annual meeting.

The Management Committee has wide powers under the Regulations. They, or any Commission or sub-committee appointed by them, can investigate the financial arrangements between all clubs and players, and check any alleged breaches of Regulation by clubs, players or officials.

The Regulations allow the Management Committee to take whatever action they may think fit. They can fine, suspend or, in a serious case, even expel from The League. Clubs are prohibited from offering inducements to other clubs' players and a breach of this Regulation is punishable by The Committee, who have the power to refuse the registration of a player if they feel an inducement has been offered.

It must be apparent to you by now that the 'Shalls' and the 'Shall Nots' of the Regulations give almost a biblical connotation to the professional game. Let us look at some of the Commandments:

> Public statements by club officials of their interest in a player of another club are regarded as an inducement within the meaning of the Regulations.
>
> All transfers of registration, and contracts of service, must be arranged directly between the clubs concerned and the player – and not through, or by, an agent.
>
> It is illegal for any club, official or player to offer or receive a payment or any form of inducement to win, lose or draw a match.

The Regulations are quite rigid in their directions to clubs about the strengths of teams fielded in League games. A less than full-strength turn-out will lead to questions being asked by the Management Committee, and if the answers are not considered satisfactory penalties can be imposed as they think fit.

Clubs cannot arrange matches, other than League matches, until the League fixtures are settled, nor can they interfere with the fixtures of other clubs. No matches in which League clubs take part, with the exception of the FA Cup Final, can be televised live unless Management Committee permission is obtained.

The Regulations control the use of one substitute in League games, and decree that two points are awarded for a win and one for a draw, and that goal average is the deciding factor when points are equal.

The Regulations carefully lay down procedures for every eventuality to do with the playing or postponement of matches and carry this sting:

> Any club failing to fulfil a League fixture on the appointed date is liable to a fine not exceeding £5,000, in addition to which they will be dealt with as the Management Committee may determine.

Perhaps the most intricately detailed section of the Regulations is that concerning finance, and although little of it is of interest to the general reader, it is worth noting that while seats and season ticket prices are decided at the discretion of the clubs, The League stipulate the minimum ground admission prices - or, rather, the clubs do, by vote.

Few ordinary spectators are aware that one shilling of every admission paid by adult spectators - sixpence for schoolchildren - has to be paid by home clubs to the visiting club, and that the minimum cheque which can be paid over is £200.

All home clubs also have to pay four per cent of their nett gate receipts to The League. This sum is placed into a Pool Account which is equally divided between all clubs at times decided by the Management Committee.

In addition to these payments The League also credit the Pool Account with amounts calculated according to the number of spectators attending all League matches, up to a maximum of threepence per head. The Management Committee decide what this amount will be. The Pool Account is further boosted by the monies from the televising, broadcasting and filming of League matches after the deduction of facility-fee payments to the clubs whose ground facilities are used.

The League also pays the Professional Footballers' Association 10% of all fees received from the filming of League matches, and this is used by the PFA for educational, insurance and benevolent fund purposes.

The Regulations covering payments to players are equally comprehensive. They stipulate a minimum wage payable to League professionals as well as the amounts of match bonuses payable in League, League Cup and FA Youth matches.

Clubs are not allowed to make payments to players apart from those strictly laid down in their contracts. A club found guilty of making extra payments to a player or his family, either in cash or kind, could be expelled from The League, or any officials involved severely reprimanded by the Management Committee. In the case of expulsion, a club has the right of appeal at an Extraordinary General Meeting of The League.

A large section of the Regulations deals with the Registration and Transfer of players. There are four types of player in The League – professional, apprentice, amateur and associated schoolboy. The appropriate form must be registered with, and approved by, The League before any player can take part in any competition organised by The League.

In the case of professionals and apprentice players copies of their contracts of service must also be forwarded to The League's Headquarters in Lytham St Annes, and the appropriate forms must be in at The League offices at least 48 hours before the player is eligible to play in a League match.

A player between his 15th and 17th birthdays, who is not a pupil of a recognised school can be registered as an apprentice up to his 18th birthday. When an apprentice is 18 he must decide whether he wishes to sign as a professional for the club for which he is registered as an apprentice, or whether he will automatically revert to amateur status. If he does this he cannot sign a registration form, or play for a professional club for two years, except with the consent of the club for which he was registered as an apprentice.

Manchester City goalkeeper Harry Dowd signs transfer forms with Football League assistant secretary Eric Howarth.

If a player who is registered as an apprentice applies to his club for cancellation of registration during his apprenticeship, he may revert to his amateur status but he cannot subsequently sign a registration form or play for a club for two years.

There is a minimum and maximum weekly wage for apprentices with the provision that the club may also pay the cost of lodgings, but cannot pay this direct to the player. The player must also be allowed to continue his further education or take up vocational training.

The associated schoolboy scheme which was agreed between The Football Association, The English Schools' Football Association and The Football League, allows clubs to sign – for the purposes of training and coaching – schoolboys who are over 13 on September 1 in any season, subject to the following conditions:

Priority at all times must be given to any school and/or schools' organisation activities.

Only boys over 15 years of age on September 1 may play for a club.

Boys over the age of 15 on September 1 may play for a club only with the permission of their headmaster or headmistress.

A boy can only be registered as an associated schoolboy for one club at a time.

Clubs are restricted in the number of schoolboys they can have registered at any one time.

The form of registration has to be signed by his parent or guardian and by the headmaster or headmistress of the school which he attends.

A club must not induce a schoolboy to leave school prematurely to sign as an apprentice player.

Now let us examine the carefully worded main points of the Regulations as they affect the players.

Any professional player whose registration is cancelled, or who is released by his club on the grounds of permanent disability, cannot be registered for any other club without the consent of the club which last held his registration. Any professional player who has applied for, and been paid the money standing to his credit in the Provident Fund, or who has received the permanent total disablement payment from the Football League Personal Accident Insurance scheme, shall not again be registered for any club.

Registrations of professional players may be transferred from one club to another only on the official League transfer form which has to be signed by the professional player and the two clubs concerned.

It is the responsibility of the club seeking the transfer of a player to satisfy themselves as to the player's fitness. The completion of the transfer form confirms that they have done this and the transferring club is absolved from any further liability.

When the registration of a player is transferred The League have to receive the duly completed transfer form, a copy of the contract of service, and a copy of the terms and conditions of all transfers of registrations. There is no fixed maximum transfer fee, but no transfer is registered until the Management Committee are satisfied that an appropriate fee has been paid or its payment adequately secured.

Temporary transfers of registrations are only approved for a defined period, subject to the conditions of such temporary transfer being made known to the player, and approved by the Management Committee. The Management Committee will not normally approve more than two temporary transfers from or to any club in any one season.

After a date in March in each season registrations and transfers of registrations may be declined, or will only be approved subject to any limitations and restrictions which the Management Committee determine. A player is eligible to play only in matches for which permission is granted by the Management Committee.

Any club playing an unregistered player in a League match may have two points deducted from its total and/or be liable to any other penalty the Management Committee decide.

If a club offers a registered amateur player professional terms which the Management Committee considers reasonable, and which the player has refused, then the registration of the player will not be accepted for another League club except by the special consent of the Management Committee.

The registration of an amateur player may only be terminated during the season by mutual consent of club and player, or by the Management Committee, if the player is not played in the class of match which his ability warrants – or for other reasons satisfactory to the Management Committee.

All contracts of service between clubs and professional players, and all fees paid for transfers, are private and confidential. No sum can be paid or received by a club for the transfer of any amateur player, unless his status is being changed to that of professional.

A professional player may, at any time during the three months before his 18th birthday, give notice in writing to the Secretary of the club employing him up to that time, that he desires to negotiate a new contract of service with the club. The club may give similar notice to the player.

Registrations of professional players and apprentices of a club ceasing to be a full member or associate member of the League are automatically taken over by the Management Committee who, at their own discretion, assess the fees to be placed on the transfers of such registrations.

The fees from these transfers go to the League. The Management Committee have the power to make a grant to the club ceasing its membership (providing it has performed all its obligations) of whatever amount of the money they think fit.

Finally, a section of the Regulations deals with miscellaneous instructions on a variety of subjects. For example, during the close season clubs have to register details of their colours (shirts, shorts and stockings) with League Headquarters. During the season no changes of colours are permitted except where colour clashes occur.

Goalkeepers in League games are only permitted to play in scarlet, royal blue, royal green or white jerseys. Their shorts and stockings must be in the registered colours of the club. No Club is allowed to play in coloured shirts which could cause confusion with the outfits worn by the match officials, that is black or dark blue are prohibited.

Each club registers its ground with The League and is not permitted to remove to another without the consent of the Management Committee. The kick-off time for League matches is fixed by the home club, but Saturday matches must not be later than 3.15 p.m. in normal circumstances. Mid-week League matches must not start later than 7.45 p.m. except by arrangement with the visiting club, and with the consent of the Management Committee.

Clubs must incorporate in any agreement with their employees an undertaking on the part of the employee to seek the permission of the club before contributing to the press, television or radio. It is the responsibility of the club to ensure that any permission granted is not used by the employee in such a way as to bring The League or any club into disrepute.

The fees paid to Referees and Linesmen are 10 guineas and 5 guineas respectively, plus stipulated expenses. It is a serious offence for a club or official, or any other person, to offer or pay to a referee or linesman more than his fee, allowances and legitimate expenses.

Match officials must normally be present at their appointment at least three-quarters of an hour before the advertised kick-off time. During the months of November, December, January and February the referee must visit the ground two hours before the advertised time of kick-off.

These, then, are the main points from The Regulations, which are moulded and amended by the clubs themselves, and on which the strength and resilience of the League edifice is founded.

Players of the Year

Bobby Charlton is Managers' Star Choice

Bobby Charlton, man of a record 106 England caps, is the Footballer of this and practically every other year of the last decade.

The taciturn, but always placid and modest Manchester United star is the player whom the experts have voted as the Footballer of the 1969–70 season. We went to The Football League club managers for our votes and asked each one: who are the top five players of the year?

They were asked to name the five – other than a player with their own club – who contributed most to the game. Playing skills, individual performances, contributions to team demands, and sportsmanship, were all facets which each was asked to take into consideration.

Bobby Charlton was the managers' star Choice. Of 66 forms returned, Charlton was nominated on 53 of them – almost twice as often as anyone else except Billy Bremner.

Every time a player was nominated to Number One spot on a manager's voting paper he was given five points. For second choice he received four points, three for third, two for fourth and one point for fifth place.

The top five players of the season, according to the experts, were:

1.	Bobby Charlton (Manchester United)	148 points.
2.	Billy Bremner (Leeds United)	122
3.	Alan Ball (Everton)	84
4.	Bobby Moore (West Ham United)	53
5.	George Best (Manchester United)	52

The next five places in the poll went to: 6. Gordon Banks (Stoke City) 47; 7. Dave Mackay (Derby County) 34; 8. Jimmy Greaves (West Ham United) 32; 9. Geoff Hurst (West Ham United) 28; 10. Emlyn Hughes (Liverpool) 26.

In all a total of 85 players were included on the 66 forms. All the top places, as was to be expected, went to players with First Division clubs.

But a large number of votes were also cast for players from the lower divisions, and we are able to nominate the Managers' Choice for all the other Divisions:

Division Two – Don Rogers (Swindon Town), Player of the year; runner-up, Alan Woodward (Sheffield United).

Division Three – Tommy Taylor (Orient), Player of the year; runner-up, Jimmy Conway (Fulham).

Division Four – Jimmy Melia (Aldershot), Player of the year; runner-up, Nigel Cassidy (Scunthorpe).

It is planned to make the Managers' Players of the Year an annual event in the Football League Book.

For the record the names of the managers who voted are appended. Each was managing a club on March 7, 1970, when the vote was taken, and the names are given in the alphabetical order of their clubs in the Football League Handbook beginning with Division One:

Harry Potts, Dave Sexton, Bert Head, Brian Clough, Harry Catterick, Bobby Robson, Don Revie, Bill Shankly, Joe Mercer, Sir Matt Busby, Matt Gillies, Danny Williams, Tony Waddington, Alan Brown, Alan Ashman, Ron Greenwood, Bill McGarry, Stan Cullis, Eddie Quigley, Les Shannon, Nat Lofthouse, Alan Dicks, Jimmy Scoular, Bob Stokoe, Eddie Firmani, Ian Greaves, Cliff Britton, Stan Anderson, Benny Fenton, Ron Saunders, Gerry Summers, George Smith, Bobby Seith, Les Allen, John Harris, Fred Ford, Johnny Steele, Freddie Cox, Freddie Goodwin, Bill Dodgin (snr), Les Hart, Lawrie McMenemy, Bill Dodgin (jnr), Basil Hayward, Alec Stock, Tommy Eggleston, Jimmy Bloomfield, Allan Brown, Dave Russell, Bill Moore, Jimmy Melia, Ken Roberts, Dick Graham, Ernie Tagg, Ray Yeoman, Johnny Newman, Bobby Kennedy, Ron Gray, Jim Iley, Gordon Lee, Ron Ashman, Ernie Shepherd, Brian Doyle, John Neal, Tom Johnston and Noel Cantwell.

BOBBY CHARLTON
(Manchester United)

The most respected footballer in Britain and the best-known British footballer throughout the world. Born in Ashington, Northumberland, he joined United as a junior on October 11, 1954, and came through their junior ranks. A survivor of the Munich air disaster Bobby has won League, FA Cup and European Cup honours with his club and was nominated Footballer of the Year by the Football Writers' Association in 1965–6. Has also won the European Footballer of the Year nomination. During the 1970 World Cup Competition in Mexico he passed Billy Wright's record 105 caps for England. At the start of the 1970–71 season his aggregate stood at a new record 106.

WHAT THE MANAGERS SAY

Ron Greenwood (West Ham United): 'Bobby has all the qualities one looks for in a top player – sportsmanship, application, endeavour and unlimited skill. Over the last decade he ranks as the most consistent player in the game.'

Bobby Robson (Ipswich Town): 'He possesses skill and technique in abundance, plus an amazing tolerance for other players. He is a model for every young player to follow.'

Harry Catterick (Everton): 'Bobby is the complete professional. A superb midfield player, he is also one of the few also able to strike at goal from any position. His utter dedication to the team and to his individual contribution – plus his respect for all opponents – make him outstanding.'

BILLY BREMNER
(Leeds United)

The driving force behind Leeds United's surge for the game's top honours. Bremner has added maturity and rigid self-control to his infectious enthusiasm and tremendous ability. Chosen Footballer of the Year for 1969–70 by the Football Writers' Association, he is the type of player every manager would like in his side – a born leader, a superb competitor and a skilled technician.

WHAT THE MANAGERS SAY

Bill Shankly (Liverpool): 'He has everything – flair, guts and brains plus that most important something . . . the will to win. A great player in anyone's book.'

Joe Mercer (Manchester City): 'Billy has harnessed his firebrand nature to become a truly great player. Physically and morally brave, like Alan Ball, he can often make the difference between winning and losing.'

Dave Sexton (Chelsea): 'Bremner combines the two facets of the game which are vital if a side is to keep winning: he is prepared to fight hard, and he can produce elegance on the ball in the most difficult situations.'

ALAN BALL
(Everton)

The man who never stops running, whether it be in a Royal Blue Everton shirt or the white shirt of England. He carved his name indelibly into the memories of millions with his displays for England in the World Cup in 1966. Allied to his technical skill, Ball possesses those priceless twin assets of stamina and will-to-win. He was developed by Blackpool and moved to Everton soon after the World Cup four years ago. At Goodison his appetite for hard work played a major part in the club's championship success.

WHAT THE MANAGERS SAY

Bill Shankly (Liverpool): 'He's the brain box in every side he plays for. Alan has the talent to get the best out of everyone around him.'

Les Shannon (Blackpool): 'He is never hard to find on the field. Alan is always in the right place, in the thick of things. His drive and competitive spirit so often means the difference between victory and defeat.'

Brian Clough (Derby County): 'Alan Ball typifies everything a manager looks for in a player. It is as simple as that.'

BOBBY MOORE
(West Ham United)

Captain of club and captain of England, Moore possesses commanding qualities of leadership given to few players. A tremendous ability to read a game allows him to anticipate as few other players and his defensive quality is extremely high. Immaculate distribution of the ball compensates for a slight lack of mobility for which he is sometimes criticised. A late choice for the 1962 World Cup he has been a permanent fixture in the national side ever since, a fact the critics might care to note. He has climbed the winner's rostrum at Wembley three times . . . for the FA Cup, the European Cup Winners' Cup and the World Cup.

WHAT THE MANAGERS SAY

Alec Stock (Luton Town): 'He is about the best distributor of the ball in the modern game. He can get it cleanly away from any angle or situation. Always composed, he is the player above all to wrap it up at the back.'

Sir Matt Busby (Manchester United): 'An ideal leader who always sets an example by his football. Tremendous defensive qualities with an uncanny ability to read the game split seconds before the opposition.'

Joe Harvey (Newcastle United): 'With Moore in your side you have a defensive artist who can lock up at the back while his ability to read ahead and to get the ball away on a slide-rule means midfield dominance.'

GEORGE BEST
(Manchester United)

The most exposed footballer of all time, an individualist and ball artist who is acknowledged by the experts as a near genius. Footballer of the Year and European Footballer of the Year honours have been bestowed on him in a period when blanket defence and team tactics have tended to stifle individualism. His brilliance is a by-word in the game, his idolators outside it are legion. Whether he blossoms into the top star of all time, the experts argue, depends on whether he can harness his magic to team responsibility . . . and on just how great his outside pressures become.

His earning power in spheres outside the football peripheral make him the first British footballer who has broken through to successfully master a widening range of activities independent of a footballing foundation. It remains to be seen how this involvement will affect him mentally and physically in the footballing atmosphere.

WHAT THE MANAGERS SAY

Bill Shankly (Liverpool): 'George is a brilliant player who can be completely untouchable on his day.'

Bill McGarry (Wolves): 'He is a player who typifies pure genius. Is there anything else to say?'

Harry Catterick (Everton): 'A player of undoubted genius whose ball control is uncanny. He can stop, and change pace, in a split second and this enables him to pull out the completely unexpected.'

DIVISIONAL PLAYERS OF THE YEAR

Second Division

DON ROGERS
(Swindon Town)

At a time many people were saying natural wingers were a dying race, Rogers has showed that there is still room in any soccer formation for a flanker with speed and skill. Developed by manager Bert Head at Swindon, Rogers – born at Paulton, Somerset, has stayed loyal to the Wiltshire club. He starred in Swindon's 1969 League Cup triumph and has won Under-23 and Football League representative honours.

WHAT THE MANAGERS SAY

Bobby Robson (Ipswich Town): 'He is a player of tremendous talent and skill, yet one who plays strictly within the spirit and laws of the game. He is as good as anyone in the lower divisions . . . and better than many at the top.'

Les Allen (Queen's Park Rangers): 'He is one of the few players left who is willing and able to commit a full back.'

Brian Clough (Derby County): 'Forwards are a difficult breed to find, left wingers are well nigh impossible. He is the type of number eleven every manager searches for.'

DIVISIONAL PLAYERS OF THE YEAR

Third Division

TOMMY TAYLOR
(Orient)

He has the potential to become one of the top names of the Seventies – that is the verdict of many managers who have cast envious eyes at this young Orient defender. Born at Hornchurch, Essex, Taylor signed for Orient in October 1968 and has already won England Youth honours. Despite his youth, he is not yet 20, he has shown a steady maturity and developing skill in his first season of League football.

WHAT THE MANAGERS SAY

Alec Stock (Luton Town): 'Remembering his age, Taylor is already a fine player, has tremendous potential. His command at the back resembles Bobby Moore in many ways.'

Dick Graham (Colchester United): 'As one of the people who helped him in his early days at Orient, it has given me a big thrill to see him develop. He has always stood head and shoulders above other lads of his age.'

Ron Gray: 'I have been chasing young players most of my career and it is not often I can say after only a few minutes that "here is one for the book". I said it when I saw Taylor.'

DIVISIONAL PLAYERS OF THE YEAR

Fourth Division

JIMMY MELIA
(Aldershot)

At Liverpool, Wolves and Southampton Melia developed into one of that exclusive band of players – the midfield general with the ability to control the course of a game. After many years at the top, during which he won England caps against Scotland and Switzerland, he moved in November 1968 to direct the fortunes of Aldershot, taking on the additional responsibilities of player-manager. His influence on and off the field has much to do with the club's revival and their fine F A Cup run last season.

WHAT THE MANAGERS SAY

Arthur Rowley (Southend United): 'The added responsibilities of looking after affairs off the field as well as on it are tough, as I found out at Shrewsbury. But Jimmy has thrived on it and he is an adaptable player, to boot, who has thrived on Fourth Division demands. Take him out of the side and it is like a ship without a rudder'.

Lawrie McMenemy (Doncaster Rovers): 'Knowing how hard it is to manage and play as well it is apparent to me what a tremendous influence he has on his players on the pitch. His skill, and sheer enthusiasm, are infectious'.

A Passionate Love for Football

— that's the Bobby Charlton secret

HARRY BROWN

The price of fame is perhaps the only part of his fabulous life as a world-renowned footballer which Bobby Charlton isn't too sure about.

Adulation isn't something which sits too easily on the shoulders of the retiring, even shy, family man whose modest charm and model behaviour on and off the pitch have made him the hero of people who are not even sure whether Association Football is played with a round or oval ball.

He told me, in the comfort of the tastefully furnished lounge of the detached home he has built in the Cheshire countryside: 'I long to be able to go to the pictures without getting embarrassed by well-wishers, but I can't. I would really like to go into a tea shop, or a restaurant, without someone pointing me out. Even when I'm driving my car the heads turn, the fingers point.'

The man who this last summer in Mexico broke Billy Wright's record of 105 England caps doesn't argue that people young and old haven't a right to want to 'chat him up', ask him for autographs or pictures, or just stare at him.

'I owe my life to them,' he is quick to point out. 'Without the supporters I wouldn't be able to make a good living playing football, which I love.' But he wonders why he can't go on the beach near the little place he has bought in Anglesey without being mobbed by youngsters – as he was last year. 'Bobby wouldn't chastise them, or push them away,' explains wife Norma, 'but he does yearn sometimes just to be able to get us away somewhere where no-one knows him.' That's why they've given up Majorca holidays ... or anywhere else in the Mediterranean sun. 'The most unlikely people turn out to be football fanatics,' they grimace.

Doesn't he, deep down, enjoy it all? After a few minutes in Charlton's company you realise he is grateful that football is so popular ... that people like himself are boosted into national figures.

'You know, I don't regard myself as an entertainer at all. I am a footballer, and that's different. I'd like to be able to leave all the so-called glamour right there where it belongs, on the pitch. But I know I can't, so I must accept that people will be curious about me.

'I firmly believe a footballer has to be completely dedicated to the game, to his training . . . that he has to pay attention to the detail of his job just like any professional man. That's why I haven't become involved in business. My Club pays me very good money to be good at my job, and I do everything I can to give them their full moneysworth.'

He is not, by inference, criticising other players whose outlook is different. 'I can only speak for myself, react according to my own nature.'

And he has a retiring nature. 'Don't get me wrong, crowds don't worry me in a football stadium. They are just a crowd to me. But I'm not so happy when they become individual faces at dinners or social events, or when I have to make pleasant conversation. I'm not at ease then.'

He remembers the occasion, soon after he had made United's senior side after signing for them in 1953, when he had to speak at a presentation for the Deaf and Dumb. 'I remember asking Joe Armstrong, the scout who took me to Old Trafford, what I should do. He told me to try to string my words together, that it would get easier as time went by. He was right.'

Bobby Charlton isn't a great talker or an avid reader, he likes walking but not gardening, really enjoys a round of golf, and loves documentary programmes on television. And he has discovered a penchant for history.

'Funny, you know,' he says, 'it was years before I even bought a camera to take with me on my overseas trips. I used to go and come back, and that was that.'

But in 1969 in Mexico, the team's hotel lounge was covered with a large freize depicting famous scenes and personalities of Mexican history. 'I had been told that Hernando Cortez was the man who practically built the country up from nothing, and it was pointed out to me that this great historical character was relegated to a far corner, peeping out behind somebody's shoulder. That got me. Why reject the country's founder?'

Bobby began asking Mexican acquaintances about the man and his times. 'I was intrigued and I bought books on it when I got back.' Last winter Bobby was reading a Hammond Innes book on Cortez and Mexico.

Bobby Charlton relaxes with his wife and daughters.

That is why in Mexico last summer Bobby Charlton was often missing . . . he was out looking at historical buildings and places and piecing together the story of the Conquistadores, as the Spanish conquerors of the country were called.

'People like General Franco in Spain, and some of the South American Presidents, have fascinating stories. When I visit their countries now I shall have read up the histories, and find out the interesting things to see. After all, it's a crime to be paid to go round the world and not take an interest in the stories of the places and the people.'

That's Bobby Charlton. A man whose experiences have developed him from a lad whose home environment as a child revolved around football and little else ('my mother's three brothers Stan, George and Jim Milburn were all Leeds full backs, and her cousin Jackie Milburn of Newcastle was a star name even in those days') into a sensitive man who thinks and cares about things and people.

The Munich Disaster made, and left, a scar which will never heal and the resultant affluence of his life contrasts sharply with that of his early days, and the lives of so many of those who revere him. 'I don't like the small people, the hangers-on, the bright-lights-brigade,' he says. 'I'm still

very much concerned with everyone getting a chance to have a happy life, but I'm sorry I didn't work harder in my schooldays. I didn't like French, for example, but how I'd like to speak it now! I can make myself understood, just about, in French but had I taken the trouble earlier, I could have mastered it.'

The Manchester United and England star would be the first to admit he is widening his interests, looking outward rather than inward. But his attitude to football stays exactly the same.

'I love it,' he says passionately. 'I'd play it for nothing if no-one would pay me. It has given me everything, and I owe football everything in return.'

Bobby acknowledges he is now a public figure. He is determined nothing he might do will cloud the image of the game he loves.

He and his charming wife Norma have two lovely daughters, Suzanne aged seven and Andrea aged five, a relaxing home and a contented life. 'I guess in the end it is his home life which makes a footballer tick at the top as long as I have. No matter what talents he might have, this is a must. I'm lucky to have that.'

Lucky? Far from it. What Bobby Charlton has, and is, he has worked for.

Gordon Banks—The Model Professional

BOB BALDWIN

The man who lives in the corner house on a modern estate deep in the rolling Shropshire countryside, a few miles from Market Drayton, is no different from any other family man.

If the weather is fine he will be out cleaning his car or tending his neat, well-kept garden - paying special attention to the rose bushes growing round the front lawn. He may even kick a ball about with his son in a field a few yards from his front door.

But on Saturday afternoons this family man is different from most others. Then he will be far removed from the peace and quiet of the countryside - he will be keeping goal for Stoke City with the label of the world's number one goalkeeper firmly attached to his broad shoulders.

The two worlds of Gordon Banks are only fifteen minutes apart by car, but a world of difference separates the atmosphere of Stoke's Victoria Ground from his home life.

'I like it this way,' says England's most-capped goalkeeper: 'As far as I am concerned football life and family life are in no way connected. That is the way I aim to keep it.'

'That's why we settled for a house in the country, far removed from the busy City life.'

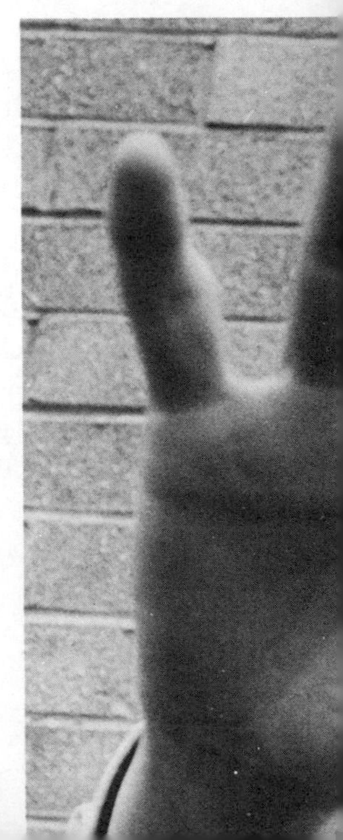

England and Stoke City goalkeeper Gordon Banks.
These are the hands which keep out the goals.

Talk to Gordon in the comfort of his home and you begin to realise how he manages that total equanimity on the field, almost unique among goalkeepers who need razor sharp reactions and are usually extroverts. Not Banks . . . he displays just the same free-and-easy approach to life when at home with his wife Ursula, son Robert, and daughters Wendy and Julia.

Is it a carefully concocted façade, or does Gordon Banks possess nerves of steel that insulate him from the tensions and pressures of life at the top?

He explains: 'I am as tense as the next man before a game, but tension in the dressing room is vital for a player worth his salt. It shows he is keyed up for the job on hand. Once on the field it is different, the butterflies soon go.' Banks grinned when his 11-year-old son Robert announced he does not play in goal because: 'there isn't enough work to do.' Replies Dad, 'If only it was as easy as that.'

Yet he finds it fairly easy to relax after a game. His wife agrees: 'Very rarely does he appear keyed up.'

Gordon says philosophically: 'I know that I will have bad days, along with the good ones, and I was told a few years ago to keep football problems as far away as possible from home life. This I have always tried to do, and it has helped to ease the pressure.'

Gordon is eager to talk about his profession, no matter where he is, no matter what he may be doing. 'They say "keepers are born and not made,", and it's true up to a point, but it is a specialist position. A

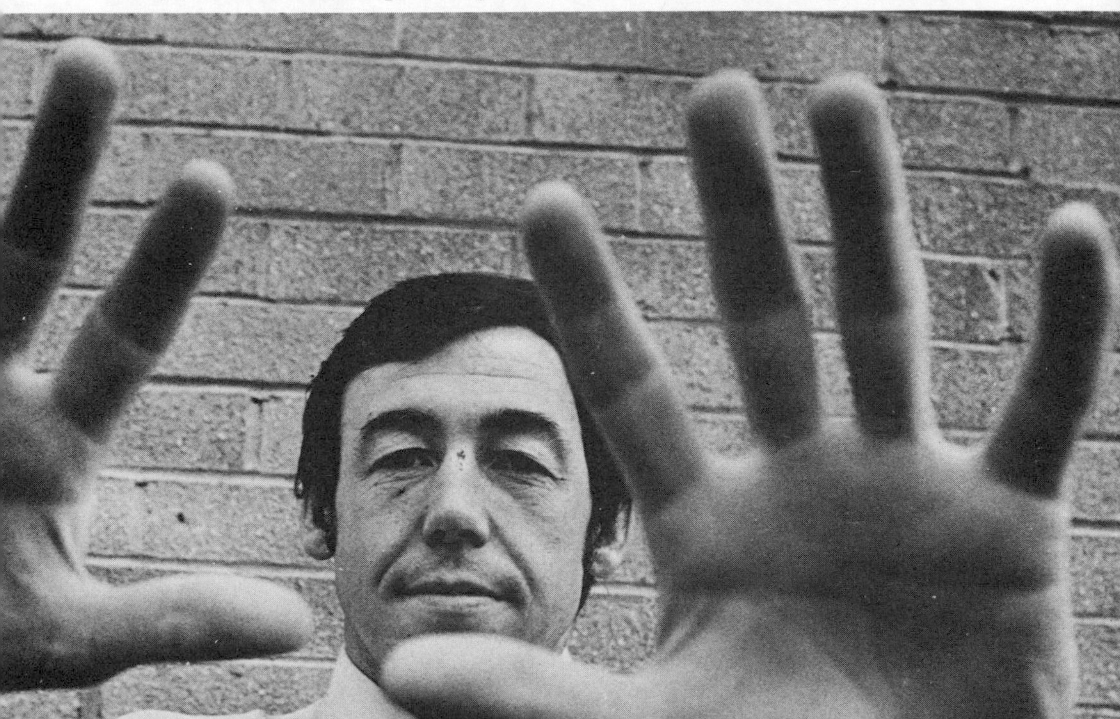

goalkeeper never stops learning his trade. People talk about new developments and styles for forwards and defenders, yet a goalkeeper's job is changing just as dramatically.'

'It is a lot harder these days than it was ten years ago. Then wingers were orthodox and you could expect the same type of ball from every cross. Today you find one may be driven hard and low towards the near post, the next is a high one for the big men in the middle. It is impossible to sit back and say you know it all.'

Despite so many years in the top bracket Gordon Banks still likes to look back to his youth – to the days when he used to carry sacks of coal after leaving school, and the training he underwent as a bricklayer. He recalls his first introduction to goalkeeping as a boy in his native Sheffield – 'I only played in goal because no-one else would.'

Individual games played long before he ever dreamed of wearing the yellow England jersey are still vivid in his memory. He talks enthusiastically about an FA Youth Cup Final for Chesterfield against a Manchester United side which included Bobby Charlton, Wilf McGuiness and Alex Dawson.

Stored away among his personal recollections are individual saves he made – and 'sitters' he let in. 'There was a save against Newcastle last season when I tipped over a header from Wyn Davies at point blank range . . . I was really pleased with that. And there were two matches for Leicester in the 1964 League Cup Final against Stoke.'

But even the greatest of artists have nightmare moments. For Banks it was a goal he conceded at Stamford Bridge in his Leicester City days. 'I never need reminding. George Eastham was playing for Arsenal at the time and was watching from the stands. He still talks about it too. There was a high ball, and no-one within twenty yards of me. I went out for a straightforward jump and catch – and the ball slipped through my hands and rolled gently over the line.'

Football has taken him to the four corners of the world and brought him fame and fortune. He makes no bones about being grateful for it.

'When I feel I can no longer contribute my best as a player I would like to turn to coaching. Maybe I'll be able to put something back into soccer.'

Gordon Banks is the model professional who has never allowed success to supersede an utter involvement, dedication and modesty.

Perhaps that's why most professionals everywhere agree he's the greatest goalkeeper of the modern football era.

Roy Sproson—Sportsman of the Season

Last season Gillette Industries introduced a monthly Sportsmanship Award Scheme in conjunction with Football League Review. Football fans were asked to send in examples of sporting acts and attitudes of players in all divisions. At the end of the season the editor of Review headed a panel which sifted through hundreds of letters in search of the man to be awarded the Sportsman of the Season accolade for which Gillette gave a prize of a £500 holiday for two in Mexico at World Cup time. Winner was Roy Sproson of Port Vale. Here we tell his story.

Mrs Joyce Sproson admits she knows very little about football. She thinks she has seen only eight matches in her life and 'don't ask me to name the opponents, I've no idea.'

It is a surprising statement from a woman whose activities revolve round the day-to-day life of a professional footballer.

Her husband Roy is the longest serving professional in the game. He signed for Port Vale in 1949 and made his 800th appearance for the Potteries club last season.

Mrs Sproson is naturally proud of her husband's achievements, even if she is not quite sure what it all means. She admits one of her more pleasant household chores is polishing a silver salver presented to Roy by the club's supporters to mark his twenty-one years in the game.

The salver, bought with the proceeds of a collection from the Vale Park supporters is a memento to a dedicated professional who has remained loyal to a club whose fortunes have fluctuated as dramatically as football has changed in those twenty-one years.

'I am often asked why I stayed with Port Vale all this time when I had the opportunities to join bigger clubs,' says Roy. 'There was a time for instance, when I could have joined Liverpool but manager Freddie Steele talked me out of it and to be honest, I don't think I have regretted it.

'People may think it is strange but all my ambitions have been tied up with Vale.'

Sproson's philosophy is uncomplicated. He might have won more honours with another club but he doubts whether he would have been as

Roy Sproson began his footballing career with Port Vale in 1949 . . . and is still a key figure 21 years later, with more than 800 League and Cup games to his credit.

happy. As it is, the trophy cupboard at the Sproson's house in Stoke-on-Trent does not exactly bulge with the souvenirs of success. There is a Third Division North championship medal, various statuettes, and a piece of Staffordshire china presented by the local council to commemorate Vale's promotion to the Second Division and their FA Cup semi-final appearance in 1954.

Two of his more treasured possessions were added to the cupboard during the summer: a long service award from The League, and souvenirs of his visit to Mexico as the Sportsman of the Season. It was a reward for magnificent dedication to the game over twenty-one years.

'The game has changed a lot since I joined Vale as a part-timer during my RAF service. For the better, I think since the lifting of the maximum wage. But there are facets I do not welcome. I used to think

referees in my early days were better than those today, but now I am not so sure. It could be that today's players are less tolerant and more sensitive than when I started.

'You never saw a fist raised in anger then. I think the players today could learn a lot from watching Rugby League. Very rarely do you see their players retaliate, yet look at the pressures they are under.'

Sproson has played under seven managers at Vale Park – starting with the late Gordon Hodgson, the former Liverpool forward who signed him, down to his present 'boss' Gordon Lee. Others on the list are Ivor Powell, two stints under Freddie Steele, Norman Lowe, Jackie Mudie and Sir Stanley Matthews.

One member of the present Port Vale staff who remembers Sproson as a 'big strong lad who tackled well' is Bill Cope, now in charge of the hundred-and-one odd-job tasks behind the scenes. He was assistant trainer in Sproson's early days and recalls watching the youngster playing for the reserves soon after joining the club. 'I went back to Gordon Hodgson and told him there was a lad who was far too good for that team. I don't think Roy played many more times for the reserves,' says Bill.

When Gordon Lee took over as manager, Sproson was on the point of retiring. The new manager, realising that Sproson's experience could be vital to a young and immature side, persuaded him to play on. Now Roy has his eyes firmly set on Jimmy Dickinson's record 764 League appearances for Portsmouth.

'I would dearly like to beat that, and then I might think about hanging up my boots.'

When that time comes it will be the end of an era for the Potteries' club. Sproson is the last remaining playing link with the side that set the soccer world on fire in the 1953–4 season by reaching the FA Cup semi-final and coming within 20 minutes of holding the eventual winners West Bromwich Albion. In the same season, the club ran away with the Third Division North title and set up a defensive record conceding only twenty-one goals in forty-six games.

Roy Sproson, an integral part of the defence still meets and chats with other players from that side. Many are now in business in the Stoke area and they regularly chat over old times at re-unions and charity games.

Despite the fact that he has never played in the First Division, Sproson has played with and against some of the game's greatest names and he lists them, 'Hagan, Mannion, Matthews, Haynes, but for me Eddie Bailey, now assistant manager at Tottenham, was among the best.'

When people talk about the tactical revolution soccer has undergone in recent years, Roy sits back and smiles. 'I will admit training is vastly different, we rarely saw a ball between matches. But tactics on the field have not altered all that much. We were playing a 4 – 2 – 4 system under Freddie Steele back in the early fifties. The only difference was it was called a defensive game.'

Physical fitness is Sproson's explanation for his long career. He admits his secret is constant activity, particularly during the close season. 'That way it is never so bad when the serious training begins again.'

During recent summers Roy has delivered milk to help him keep active; he also points to the do-it-yourself jobs he has undertaken at home. ‘I remember early season training not so long ago when I really began to feel my age. I was on the verge of packing it all in when I looked round and saw one of the youngsters, he couldn’t have been more than twenty, being physically sick in a corner of the field. That helped me find a second wind.’

Roy Sproson may have missed out on the big time but he has no regrets. ‘I have always loved the game and I have always loved the club. The satisfaction of playing the game I love for the club I love has always been enough for me.’

How the League Does Its Housekeeping

Just like anyone else The Football League has to do its housekeeping, has to pay its bills, its rates and taxes.

The League is a limited liability Company and is treated just like any other company when it comes to taxation on its profits, but The League is also different. It is **not** a profit-making concern, in the accepted normal understanding of the phrase.

Its object, after paying the administrative expenses of running The League, is to distribute surplus income to the member clubs. But this is not as simple to achieve as its sounds.

All the income it receives is taxable, but payments made to clubs by a direct distribution of such income does not count as an expense of The League. In other words, ways and means have to be found to distribute money to the member clubs which will not attract taxation.

It has been done.

The main income of The Football League is the sale of the Copyright of its fixtures. In 1959 there was a case in the High Court which

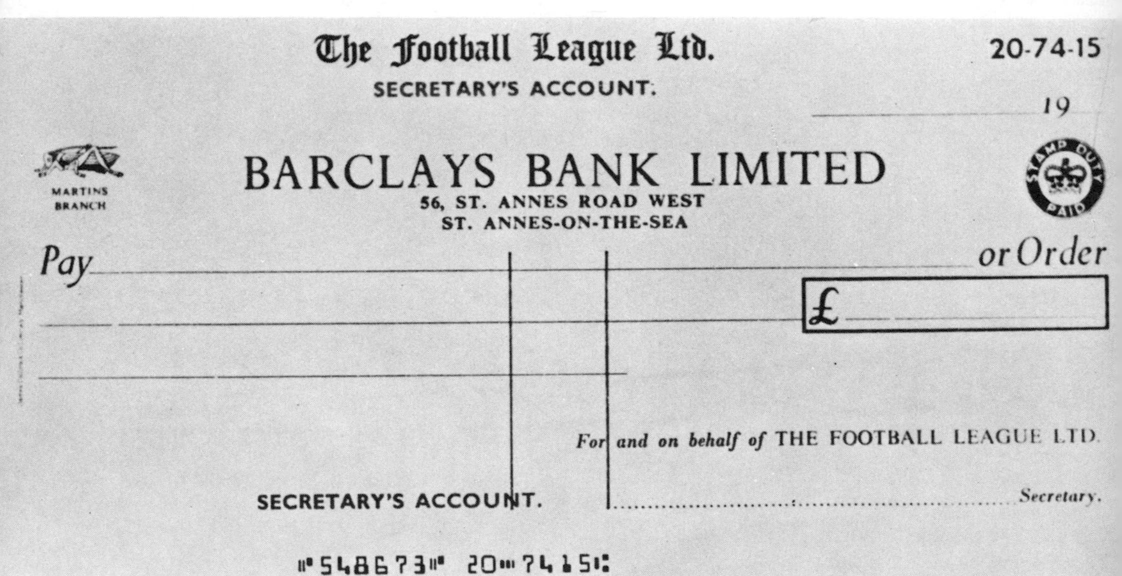
The Football League Ltd.
SECRETARY'S ACCOUNT.
20-74-15
19
MARTINS BRANCH
BARCLAYS BANK LIMITED
56, ST. ANNES ROAD WEST
ST. ANNES-ON-THE-SEA
STAMP DUTY PAID
Pay or Order
£
For and on behalf of THE FOOTBALL LEAGUE LTD.
SECRETARY'S ACCOUNT.
Secretary.
⑈548673⑈ 20⑆74 15⑆

established that the Fixture Lists of The Football League were Copyright. Since that date the main income has been derived from the sale of the fixtures to the Pools organisations, fixed odds bookmakers, and various other concerns who use the fixture lists for advertising purposes.

The total income received from this source is something more than half a million pounds each year.

After paying their administrative expenses The League distribute this to the Member clubs by the following methods:

Player's Personal Accident Insurance Scheme

The League pay a premium of £165,000 each year to cover the players registered with The Football League for Personal Accident Insurance. The total cover under this scheme is in excess of £13 million, and is allocated between the 92 clubs in the ratio of their wage bill. Clubs are then covered in respect of any incapacity to their players caused by accident, either for temporary disablement or permanent disablement. The cover not only includes footballing accidents. It also provides clubs with a 24-hour cover on their players against any accident sustained at any time.

Referees' and Linesmen's Fees and Expenses

The expenses and fees of the referee and linesmen at each League match are paid by the home club at the end of matches. The

League accountant Norman Thomas working on League books.

club then sends a return to The Football League and is reimbursed. The total amount paid in a season is now in excess of £100,000.

Contribution to Percentage Pool Account.

The balance of The League's income is distributed to clubs by means of payments to a Percentage Pool Account which will be explained later. This contribution is based on a payment per head of spectators attending Football League matches. At the present time this contribution is 1½d per head, and totals something in the region of £180,000 per year.

In addition to this income The League administers other finance through what is known as 'Mutuality pools' of which there are three:

The Percentage Pool Account

Four per cent of the nett gate of all League and League Cup matches is paid to The League, to which is added the contribution paid by The Football League as I have already mentioned. Also paid into this account are the Television and Broadcasting fees which are received by The League. At the end of each season the total amount is divided equally between the 92 clubs.

The Football League Cup Pool

In the League Cup Competition 20 per cent of each gate is paid into a Cup pool. This is also divided equally at the end of the season between clubs who participated in the competition. Last season, for the first time, all 92 clubs competed.

The Football Association Cup Pool

This is really administered by the FA. One-third of the gate money at each FA Cup match, from the Third Round onwards, is paid by the Football Association into this pool. At the end of each season the FA pay this money to The League who, in turn, distribute it among their Member Clubs.

In season 1968–9 approximately £970,000 was distributed from these three pools, so each League club received more than £10,000 from this source.

What other 'housekeeping' accounts are there?

The Football League Provident Fund. Since 1949 The League has run the Provident Fund for all players registered with The League. Each year a player has credited to him a percentage of his earnings and this is invested in the form of an insurance policy, which is paid out when he reaches 35, or retires as a League player, whichever is the later.

The fund has certain restrictions which are laid down by the Inland Revenue. No player who earns over £2,000 in any particular year can benefit in the fund in that year, and the maximum premium a player can receive in one year is £100. The percentage of earnings at the moment is 10 per cent, and this costs The League approximately £130,000 a year.

The premium is paid for by the Signing-on Levy. When a player is transferred from one club to another 5 per cent of the transfer fee is paid to The League. There is a minimum payment of £250, and this sum is also payable in the case of a player who signs for a club for the first time.

Football League Pension Scheme. All the Secretaries, Managers, Trainers and Coaches employed by Football League clubs are members of The Football League Pension Scheme, which is administered from The League Office. Members contribute 5 per cent, and clubs 10 per cent, of their salaries into the scheme which provides retirement benefits at 65. There is also provision for a death benefit should a member die before retirement.

Finally The League runs *The Football League Review,* their official magazine which is published every week during the season and circulated to the public via programmes and match-day magazines. It has a circulation of approximately 300,000 a week, and the finances are administered in the same way as any other publication.

All this adds up to a giant housekeeping bill, one which confirms the large financial turn-over which has transformed modern professional football into a business as well as a sport.

It is not a facet of the industry which normally excites the interest of newspapers or magazines, but if ever the housekeeping bill went into the 'Red' football as we know it would cease to exist.

Footballers of the Seventies

Photographs by PETER ROBINSON

Emlyn Hughes (left) – Liverpool made a shrewd buy when they signed Hughes from Blackpool where he had made only a handful of League appearances. Today he rates as one of the top defenders in the game. Derek Dougan (Below, top picture) – Wolves' Irish international centre forward is pictured in action with Tottenham's England full back Cyril Knowles. Francis Lee (below, bottom picture) – An explosive forward for Manchester City and England, Lee has been a key figure in his club's successful drive for honours in recent seasons. Here he slopes past West Bromwich defender John Kay.

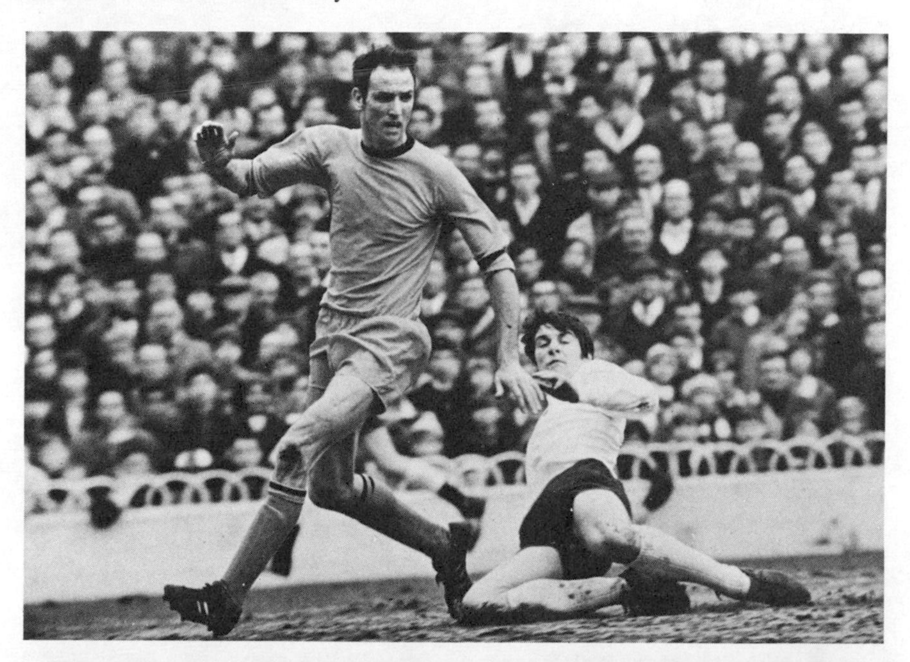

Mike England (below) – Tottenham and Wales centre half. England is rated the best pivot in the game by the men who know – the centre forwards who face him. Joe Royle – One of the reasons for Everton's League Championship success was the goal scoring form of Joe Royle, pictured (right) challenging Liverpool's Ray Clemence. Carlo Sartori – Manchester United's talented mid-field player made a big impression during the 1969–70 season, particularly during his club's epic FA Cup semi-final games with Leeds. In the picture above Sartori (centre) takes on Tottenham's Cyril Knowles.

In the full page picture, left, Bobby Graham – Liverpool's bustling young Scottish forward takes to the air as Everton's Sandy Brown slides into the tackle during a Mersey Derby. Graham won himself a regular place in the Liverpool side last season. Mike Summerbee – Manchester City's England international (below). Summerbee can prove a match winner in his own right. In this picture he takes on Ray Wilson (West Bromwich) during City's 2–1 League Cup victory at Wembley. Peter Thompson – Liverpool's winger has shown that there is still room in modern tactics for a flanker with skill and speed. Picture left, this page.

Ron Davies (above) – One of the game's outstanding scorers for several seasons, the Southampton number nine possesses all the talents of a lethal poacher and is particularly strong in the air. Geoff Hurst (below) – West Ham and England striker. Hurst earned World-wide acclaim by scoring a hat trick in the 1966 World Cup Final against West Germany and he is still one of the deadliest scorers in international football. Jack Charlton – Long serving Leeds United centre half, Charlton has scored many vital goals for United and England from the set piece moves. In this picture (full page, right) 'Big Jack' stands poised for action.

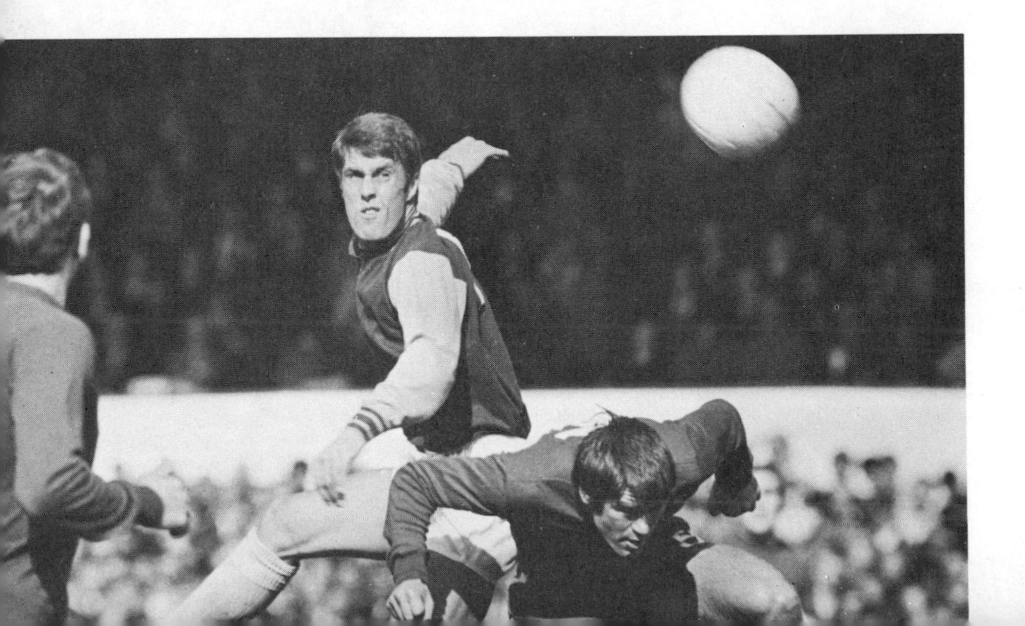

The How, Why and When of League Referees

Where do the referees and linesmen come from ... the men who officiate at the 46 Football League games every Saturday afternoon?

They come from a League pool of:

70 Referees
30 Auxiliary Referees/Linesmen
311 Linesmen.

The numbers vary from year to year and these were last season's figures, but the way they get on to The Football League list stays the same.

Let us look first at those auxiliary referees and those linesmen, for that's where the future top referees will come from. They are all men currently refereeing in leagues one step down the scale from The Football League – the Southern, Northern Premier and Central Leagues are just three examples of what are known as Contributory Leagues to The Football League list.

These officials get occasional Football League refereeing appointments to test their potential, and when they are not running a Football League line, are refereeing in their own sphere.

Their suitability for inclusion as full referees on The League list is checked by a panel of more than 40 people, all former referees of note, who are known as Football League Assessors. These men work quietly, sitting somewhere in the stands, unknown to the man under survey.

As soon as a season is completed, staff in the Referees' Office at Football League headquarters, supervised by Mr George Readle, begin their preparations for the next season. Their first task is to analyse and summarise individual performances in League games during the season just completed so that recommendations based on statistics can be made to the Football League Secretary, the Referees' sub-committee and, ultimately, The League Management Committee, as to which referees should be retained on, or deleted from, the list. A few deletions are automatic because of age – 47 is the retiring age for referees, 45 for linesmen.

Similar investigations are made into the League records of Auxiliary Referee/Linesmen. Some may be promoted to the Referees' List, some retained for a further period of assessment as Auxiliary Referee/Linesmen and others may be retained only as linesmen, but this is dependent on their being kept on their Contributory League referees' lists.

The records of the Contributory League referees, based on their Contributory League performances, are received by The Football League during May of each year and from these a number of referees are selected for inclusion on the Auxiliary/Referees/Linesmen's list the following season.

The linesmen are chosen from the other referees on Contributory League lists, but as these are not completed until later it is usually well into July before The Football League Linesmen's list is completed.

Not until the lists are complete can the task of appointing them to matches on The League fixture list begin. The appointments are made on a monthly basis and the target is to issue the list three weeks before the month starts, but even then work on it is invariably unfinished.

Amendments are constantly necessary because of illness, injury or Football Association appointments, among a variety of reasons. The complexity of the problem can be gauged from the following statistics which show the number of changes from original match appointments in the last three seasons.

	1967–8	1968–9	1969–70
Changes of match dates (for weather and other reasons)	160	299	302
Changes of referee	143	145	229
Changes of linesmen	162	218	174

Before last season it was The League's practice to appoint referees, generally, to matches within a certain radius of their homes but a system of grading has now been introduced. Referees with the better records are now appointed to officiate in the more important games in all divisions (for example, where promotion and/or relegation is involved or for the local 'derby' games). Referees may be promoted to this group during a season if their records indicate their worthiness or, conversely, they may be removed from the group if their performances show deterioration.

Until recently assessment of referees was conducted solely on the basis of club markings, but The League has now evolved a system of independent assessment. It was first tried on an experimental basis during the 1967–8 and 1968–9 seasons and was considerably extended last season.

The members of the Panel of Assessors are all former referees with experience at Football League level. There were 39 at the end of last season and it is now the intention to give assessment coverage at every League game.

In order to gain maximum benefit from the scheme the choice of the panel members has to be selective. The study of reports from present Assessors, and consideration of the merits of possible new members need careful consideration, in order that constant review ensures the best possible panel is serving the interests of the game.

One of the essential facets of the Assessment Scheme is that reports on referees should be as varied as possible, and in order to get this variety of opinion and approach every effort is made to ensure that any one referee is not judged by the same assessor more than once in one season.

Assessors' reports are carefully scrutinised and summarised in order to project the strengths and weaknesses, not only of individual referees, but to furnish a general picture of Refereeing standards which can help to solve such problems as the type of training and instruction necessary to help eliminate weaknesses.

Just like refereeing and line appointments those for the assessors are made monthly and, like them, are subject to constant amendment. There is one extra snag, too. If an Assessor was listed to check on a particular referee who subsequently pulls out, and he has already assessed the replacement, he has then to be switched to another match and a deputy found.

So referees' records are based on marks received from clubs and Assessors and the statistics are constantly checked as a season progresses. Whenever necessary referees are informed of any apparent failings, and told how and why an Assessor considers their all-round performance might be improved.

Referees must maintain a certain standard of efficiency and if they fall below that standard over a reasonable period then they are removed from the List.

What must be remembered is that, like players, referees have their good matches and their poor matches. To judge a man on one performance is always unfair, yet the majority of football supporters – or indeed the critics – have little opportunity to do otherwise.

Only one referee can be seen at a time. The League in fact, can see nearly 40 at the same time and this season hope to have informed assessment on every referee at every match.

Armed with that knowledge, and aware of the improvements recent innovations have effected, The Football League is satisfied that standards are keeping pace with the stringent requirements of our now very professional game.

Dave Smith – One of the League's best known referees in action.

Behind the Scenes

Keeping England Fit

No trainer to an international side anywhere in the world is as lucky as the England trainer. That is what England trainer Harold Shepherdson insists.

He says: 'It's a tribute to every club trainer up and down the country. No matter which club Sir Alf Ramsey may call upon it's the same . . . the player is as fit as a fiddle.

'We don't have to train them at England level, it's done for us. Sir Alf gets them just as he wants them in order to take it from there and harness this fitness to his own tactical blue-prints.'

Mr Shepherdson, who supervises the fitness of England squads, and who has attended more than 120 internationals and 12 Football League sides in this role since 1957, is delighted to pay this tribute.

'I've been all round the world, but I have never seen this fitness equalled. It makes my job so very easy.'

He also pays tribute to Middlesbrough FC for whom he signed as a player in 1936 and where he has been ever since as Assistant Trainer, Trainer, and now Assistant Manager. 'I was promoted from trainer, but Sir Alf allowed me the best of both worlds by asking me to continue in the job with England. It means a great deal of hard work and travel, but I love it. My club has never done anything but encouraged me when the calls from the FA have come. I am most grateful to them for that.'

What does an Assistant Manager do? Backed by an able administrative staff, as at Middlesbrough where club Secretary Harry Green is one of the most able men in the game, Harold's desk work is devoted mostly to player problems on which he works closely with Manager Stan Anderson.

His main labour of love is the control of scouting. 'My job is to encourage youngsters to Ayresome Park,' he explains. 'I spend many hours just watching boys and then trying to convince them that here at Middlesbrough we really care. Slowly we are building back to our rightful place in the game, and at the base of the club's recovery is the youth policy which has been finding more and more youngsters who are gradually flowing into the team. Up to now we have not quite found the material to get us into Division One, but the outlook has never been more encouraging.'

As part of his work Mr Shepherdson, awarded the M.B.E. for his part in England's football successes, talks to schools and youth clubs and generally engages in the task of building up his club's image in the locality of Ayresome Park. 'My connection with England's football team helps me and helps the club,' he explains modestly.

He spreads the Middlesbrough image by accepting invitations from far and near to talk to Referees' Societies, Youth Clubs, football coaches . . . and anyone else who wants to listen. 'It's a busy life, and a fascinating one,' he admits.

Just how busy can be illustrated by the experience of his daughter Margaret. She was thirteen last June and Harold has never yet been home for one of her birthday parties.

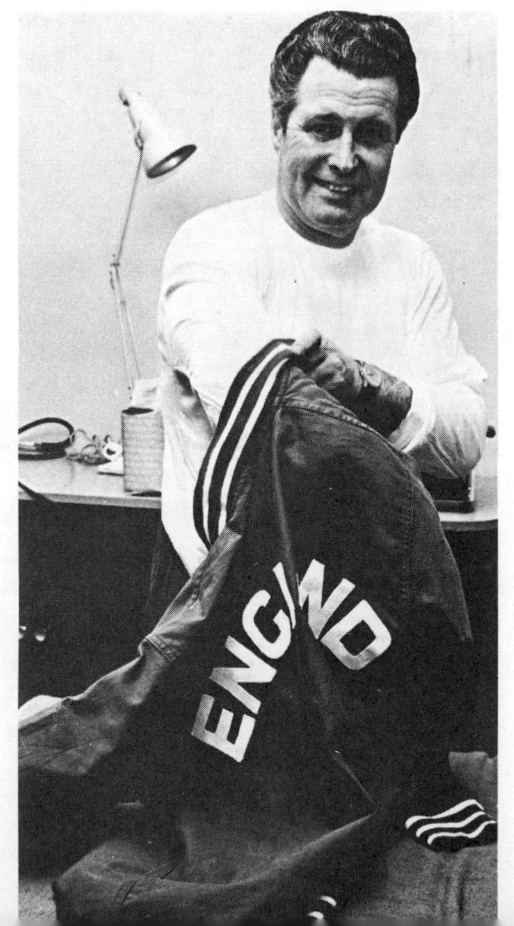

Harold tries on his England tracksuit for size before this year's international with Scotland.

This year he was in Mexico with England. 'Do you know,' he says, 'she has never complained. Like my wife and two other daughters she has always said she is only too happy to help me. You can't hope to do well in your job unless your family is with you.'*

*Harold has never had any sons but has two other daughters, Valerie and Linda, both married - the latter to Middlesbrough wing half Frank Spraggon.

Dave Exall – the Man Who Raises Money

Man cannot live by bread alone, says the Good Book. It is equally certain that no Football League club can exist solely on match receipts.

Even large and affluent clubs like Everton FC have found it vital to augment their substantial match income with monies from other sources in order to build the stylish and luxurious new accommodation now going up at Goodison Park.

There is a tremendous cash potential on the football peripheral which clubs are now learning to tap and it is the job of the Promotions Manager, Commercial Manager - call him what you will - to do just that.

Everton called in David Exall from Birmingham City just over a year ago and gave him the title of Promotions Manager. He doesn't interfere with the manager's responsibilities, nor does he intrude on the administrative field of the secretary.

He simply raises money and sets out to improve the club's public image. David Exall's first job when he arrived at Goodison in April 1969 was to ensure a regular weekly income for the club from other sources than the gate. He started a Pool which now has 2,500 agents and a weekly ticket circulation so big he won't reveal it, except to say that it is 'substantial', and that agents come from as far afield as North Wales and Dublin.

Most of them pick up their tickets, and pay in their cash, on Saturdays when the Development Office is crowded right through the day. But fifty per cent of the work is done through the post, keeping a large staff busy throughout the week.

The Pool, while the most important plank in the Promotions Platform, is far from the only task facing Mr Exall. He is also the technical

England trainer Harold Shepherdson (centre) relaxes with the cards before an England match. Players left to right are Emlyn Hughes (Liverpool), Jeff Astle (West Brom), Martin Peters (Spurs) and Alec Stepney (Manchester United).

editor of the match day magazine which he inaugurated last season. He has two journalists working under his control, with whom he discusses policy and content on Tuesdays, but the overall decisions are his and it is a job he enjoys. 'The magazine is an important link between a club and its supporters.'

His latest plank comes with the building of new offices where a magnificent Club Shop will be situated. Everton plan to sell all the usual mementos and souvenirs there and a lot more besides . . . but exactly what remains a secret.

If that sounds like a job-and-a-half (which it is) it isn't quite the lot. Mr Exall also runs the match day record programme in which he plays record requests, inserts interesting snippets about home team players and the visitors, and generally keeps up a chatty half hour which takes some beating throughout The League. 'A programme like this,' he says, 'if it is to be worthwhile has to have time and money spent on it in research. That's what we do.'

During his first year, just to ensure that his days never start at nine nor end at five, David Exall organised a new programme selling routine, bought waterproof raincoats for sellers and provided them with special feeding points for extra copies, outlined his new offices and programme collecting points in the big new stand, and saw to it that Everton had a continuous and healthy income from brand new sources.

Not bad for a first year. And a definite pointer to the way ahead for football clubs who can no longer be content with a few big pay days at the gate every season.

It's a new world. And people like David Exall are important cogs in it.

David Exall chats to a workman on site in the new £1,000,000 stand at Goodison Park.

A Sports Centre in Town

Ambitious and newly promoted Luton Town are the only club in The League to run a Sports Centre in a main shopping street and away from their ground.

Chairman Mr A. T. Hunt decided: 'We need a club shop, but we need something more than the usual souvenir and programme sales. We shall sell every kind of sports equipment, we shall sell tickets for away train and coach trips and we shall house our Development Association staff there as well.'

The club bought premises in town and last October the Sports Centre was opened. Says Manager Harry Haslam: 'The crowds flock in and the venture is a big success. When you come to think of it it's right that the League club in any area should also sell and advise on football kit and equipment and, indeed, all sports. Our players come in and serve at times and the fans see various club personalities when they visit us. The lads queue up for autographs and chat with players and officials and we think this is part of Luton Town's service to the public – it's direct

Luton Town vice chairman Mr. L. S. Hawkins (right) talks to Harry Haslam (centre) and shop manager John Wilkinson.

contact with our customers in an affiliated field, so to speak.' The shop, at 231 Dunstable Road, Luton, itself sells every conceivable item of football souvenir, sports games and equipment from boxing gloves to roller skates.

It's an eye catching experiment. And it could be a pointer to the future throughout The League.

Jim Iley - Player Manager

Until last year he had been a First Division star for most of his seventeen years as a professional. But now Jim Iley is the player-manager at Fourth Division Peterborough United.

The man who signed for Sheffield United in 1953, and who then saw service with Spurs and Nottingham Forest before a seven-year stint with Newcastle United, never watches a First or Second Division match these days, except on television.

When he isn't playing or watching his own teams he spends all his time at Third and Fourth Division games or at matches involving senior club reserve sides.

'I have to concentrate on the tactics in the Third and Fourth Divisions,' he explains. 'I can keep abreast of tactical changes in the top flight with the aid of my television set, but I have to be realistic. That isn't my world now.'

Is there, then, such a huge gap between the First and Fourth Divisions? 'Of course there is. But not the commonly accepted gap. The real class is missing, but the standard in the Fourth Division is extremely high, the entertainment value as good. But that certain something called class isn't there, and anyone who expects it to be lives in a dream world.'

Iley insists: 'It's a certain something which is difficult to define and most supporters who go to lower division matches quickly realise it isn't important to their fun. Many say there is more fun in the Fourth'.

That is as may be, and we believe Jim Iley has hit the nail on the head . . . but what is the exact difference which makes all the difference?

'It comes in the last third of the field, around the opposition's box. It is the sharpness of reaction near goal which makes the top class player. Goal grabbing is the hardest job in football and a boy who has that certain something in the penalty area is a certainty for stardom.'

Jim Iley as he was when captaining Newcastle United a couple of years ago. Note how he is running things despite being in the thick of the action.

The Peterborough player-manager pinpoints another essential gulf between the grades. 'First Division sides can adapt their tactics to the demands of the opposition. Players can quickly adapt these on the pitch to any formation necessary to overcome a tactical switch, but lower down the scale managers have to organise to a system which fits the ability of playing staffs and these have to be adhered to rigidly. There can be no fluidity about this during the game; a manager dare not chop and change because his players are unable to adapt quickly enough.'

Meanwhile Jim Iley remains one of the few men who tackles the demands of a player-manager's job within The Football League. His week is heavy and demanding and his wife and family see very little of him. In fact Friday afternoons, when he slips out to do shopping chores with his wife, provide the only real relaxation.

He trains with his team ('I don't smoke or drink so I still don't struggle and when I can't keep up with the rest I'll hang up my boots') and attends to office administration in the afternoons.

'A great deal of clap-trap is spoken and written about the difficulties of being a player as well as a manager, but players have plenty of spare time and that's when I fit in my managerial work. A man with an active mind can only find challenge in it . . . and that's how I see it.'

In his twelve months as a boss Iley has pruned the age of his side and believes he now has a team ready to challenge upwards again.

Good luck to his efforts. On and off the field.

The Secretary's Day

EDDIE PLUMLEY

There is only one certainty in any day in the normal working week of any League club Secretary . . . it will be geared to the kick-off time of the next match.

'Whatever might happen to you or your club during the day, the one target is that match,' says Coventry City Secretary Eddie Plumley. 'It is the certainty that every one of more than 2,000 League fixtures every season will be staged at exactly the right time, unless the weather intervenes, which has made The Football League the strongest and best in the world.

'It is not like that in other countries. We just do not realise in England how fantastic is the set-up here.'

But this is the Secretary's only certainty. You can't get any idea of his typical day, simply because there isn't one. 'Every day is different,' says the ebulliently efficient Coventry man. 'You arrive at nine, and you don't know what might happen next. You have to play it by ear. There could be a big transfer which has to be given priority over everything else, there might be a big match for which special arrangements have to be made and tickets printed. Perhaps there will be a crisis, about how to deal with large groups of expected visiting supporters, for example. Anything and everything happens.'

There are set routines, too. A great deal of paper-work has to be completed to satisfy Football Association and Football League Regulations. A great deal of correspondence has to be attended to, so that the liaison between club and public is fostered and maintained.

The Secretary provides the link between the Board of Directors and the public in all matters except that of the team. He is responsible in law for everything the company does within the meaning of the Companies

Eddie Plumley inspects the arrangements outside the main Coventry City entrance before the Inter-League match between the Football League and the Scottish League last March.

Plumley checks up in the City ticket office on the morning of a League match.

City laid on a Haggis treat for the Scots when the Scottish League played The Football League at Highfield road last season. Eddie Plumley inspects the Haggis: On the left is the club's Head Chef.

Act, just as he is responsible for everything the company does within the Regulations of FA and League. Meetings with club staff, as well as the public, take up so much of the time, and the phone never stops ringing. Players go to him to sort out wage questions, insurance problems, benefits, housing queries, national insurance . . . the list is endless.

At Coventry Eddie Plumley has a large staff, with whom he meets regularly to organise and delegate responsibility. With the Stadium Manager he discusses the ground and its environs and buildings, with the Catering Manager the hiring of Restaurant and other facilities, and the quality of food from the First-Class Restaurant to the Buttery Buffet. He meets the Financial Director of the club to keep abreast of club finances, and the Match Day Magazine editor to discuss programme content and policy.

'Everything simply has to tick over smoothly,' he explains. 'Mistakes can cost us friends, headaches and trouble.'

So each day is a new challenge, with new problems and, in between, normal office routine must go on. Says Mr Plumley: 'I am especially lucky at Coventry. My work is made easier by a tremendous staff. Every one a specialist, every one a round peg in a round hole.'

Perhaps that is why the facilities at Highfield Road, among the finest in the game, always catch the eye.

The people responsible for making them all work are second to none.

The Complexities of Fixture Making

DOUGLAS FLOWER

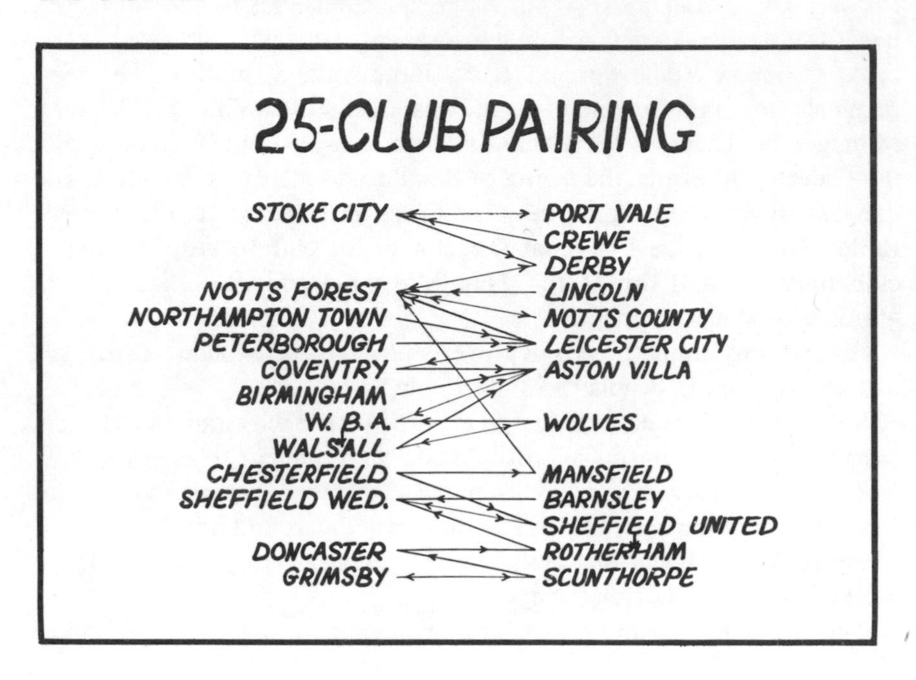

A diagram showing club "pairings" – clubs who do not want their home matches to clash. A chain effect builds up, and on this occasion last season 25 clubs were involved in a "No clashing Build up". Like to have made the fixtures for that particular Saturday?

In mid-summer every year a complete set of Football League fixtures for the following season is published. Inevitably, the criticism follows: this or that match is wrong, this or that club could have had a better deal.

But few people ever consider the searching problems facing both the League staff and the personnel at the BARIC Computing Services centre when they seek to produce fixtures week in and week out for over nine long months for 92 different clubs in four separate divisions.

Here Mr Douglas Flower, Manager of the Planning Division, explains some of the problems which have to be tackled and overcome in the fixture-making process.

It takes long months of intensive research, countless nights of burning the midnight oil, to produce the fixtures which make up a Football League season.

Their preparation involves many stages, and much stopping and starting, before the list is finally published. The first flutterings begin in the November of the year before, when the European Union of Football Associations decide on which dates in the following season the various rounds of the several European competitions will be played.

When that information is known the Secretaries of the English, Scottish, Welsh and Irish Football Associations, and Football Leagues, immediately determine the precise dates for each of their League matches and Cup rounds. The Football League – and they are the body who concern us here – then determine on which 42 days the First and Second Division clubs will play their matches, and on which 46 days the Third and Fourth Division clubs will play theirs.

At this point the dates of the eight rounds of the FA Cup, and the seven rounds of the Football League Cup, are also arranged. This scene-setting is completed by the end of January. During March the Football League sends a detailed questionnaire to its 92 clubs, involving a number of key questions. In particular, clubs are asked which other club they desire to be 'paired' with – that is when they want to be away when which other clubs are at home. That is essential first-base information.

When the fixture lists come to be finally compiled a number of other factors have also to be taken into account.

Pairings

There are the obvious cases where clubs in the same areas, such as Manchester City and Manchester United, Liverpool and Everton, Tottenham Hotspur and Arsenal, must avoid clashing with each other for home games. In addition many other clubs, particularly those in the lower Divisions, are anxious to avoid a clash with nearby First Division clubs for home games, so that their 'gates' will not be affected.

For example, Stockport County wish to 'pair' with Manchester City to avoid competition with the attraction of Maine Road (see illustration on page 107). Some of the resultant chains are very long, and illustration on opposite page shows the longest one during the 1969–70 season, when 25 clubs were involved. The arrows show various pairings which had to be considered when lists were compiled.

Without exception neighbouring clubs such as Liverpool and Everton do not clash throughout the season unless, of course, the luck of Cup draws has them both at Home on the same day. But the problems of pairings and cross-pairings desired by each individual club throughout the 92 provides enough problems on their own for fixture compilers to defeat the ambitions of any would-be critic.

Home and Away Sequences

It is important to try to arrange that clubs play alternately at Home and Away on successive Saturdays. Spectators form the habit of supporting their club every other Saturday, and a long sequence of Away matches would break this habit. The problem is considerably complicated by having to fit in mid-week matches and Cup rounds, in which only some of the Divisions have League fixtures arranged. It is not possible to arrange that every club alternates with Home and Away matches throughout the season, but the number of occasions when successive Away fixtures are allocated is kept to the absolute minimum.

Christmas Travel

It is both desirable, and functional, to keep travel to a minimum for the Boxing Day matches each season. With virtually no public transport on Christmas Day, and Sunday services operating on Boxing Day, a 'bad' fixture might mean a club had to set out on Christmas Eve to make sure of arriving at their venue on time. Because of this The League specifies the matches it wants played on this date, and rarely does a club have more than 100 miles to travel.

But because of the overall complex fixture pattern it is virtually impossible to ensure that this will **never** occur.

Special Dates

Clubs do have particular dates when they wish to play Away to avoid clashing with counter-attractions like Race Days and big Cricket matches as just two examples. Northampton Town lose the use of their ground to Northamptonshire County Cricket Club at the start and end of each season, and just cannot be allocated home matches in these periods.

It is immediately apparent that many factors have to be taken into account. You might ask 'Why can't a pattern be devised to solve the problem once and for all?' Unfortunately, in addition to the fact that there will be changes every season in the pattern of the dates on which fixtures are played, there are also promotion and relegation alterations to consider. Of the 92 clubs in the four Divisions, eight are promoted and eight are relegated every season. So even ignoring the annual question of re-election, the fact is that if football were played for another 1,000 years it is extremely unlikely the constitution of the four Divisions would be the same for any two seasons.

The real work on fixture making can only be carried out when the last of the promotion and relegation issues has been decided. As the playing season is becoming more and more crowded The Football League two years ago called in a computer to see whether it could speed up the process . . . which it has.

As each season approaches its close The League meets the computer people to discuss the following year's problems. As soon as the season is over a draft list is produced in a matter of days. This is then studied in detail, and discussed by The Football League and computer staffs.

Diagram shows a Manchester City "pairing" 1–1 meaning their home fixtures must not clash with United, should not clash with Stockport County.

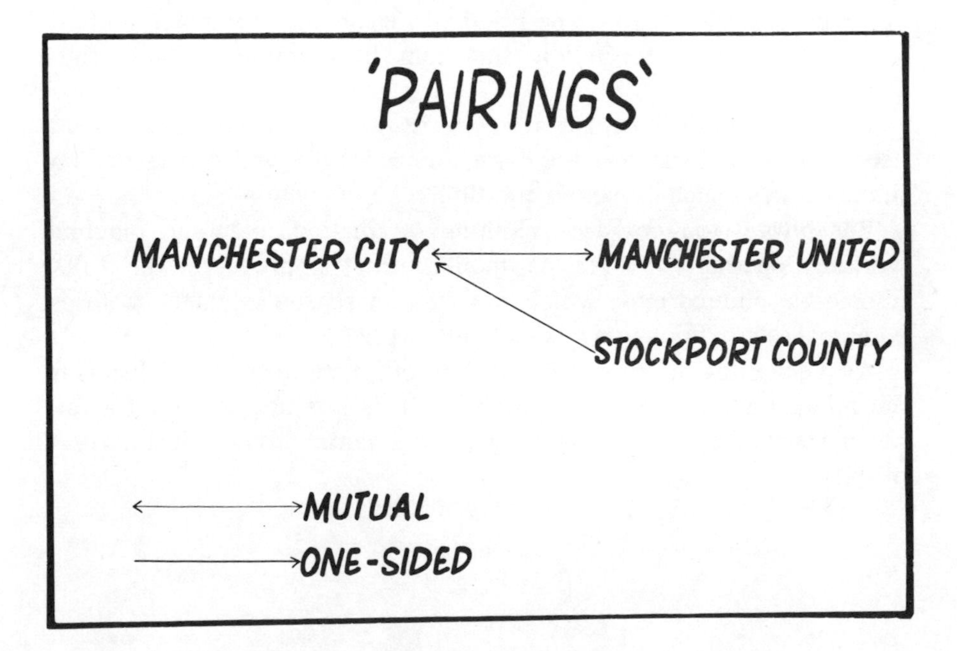

Necessary adjustments are made, and another list produced. It takes the KDF9 computer less than two minutes to produce the fixture lists from the fresh set of information fed into it, so the problem of revising the list is not time-consuming.

Only when the Fixtures have been finally accepted by The League, are they sent to all clubs for their comments. The fixtures are in their hands within a fortnight of the end of each season as a result of a lot of hard and concentrated work by The Football League staff in Lytham St Annes and the computer staff 70 miles down the M6 at Kidsgrove, not far from Stoke-on-Trent in Staffordshire.

The list also goes to the Secretaries of other Leagues who have to leave their fixture arrangements until The Football League's is completed. Because of the close tie-up, the fixtures of the Rugby League, the Central League and the Football Combination are produced on the same computer in the following few weeks.

Though it is still not possible to give every club what it wants all the time, The Football League, by making use of the speed and accuracy of the computer, is now able to meet many more individual club requests than they have ever done. The role of the computer is not that of a magician which comes up with mysterious answers, rather does it complete a mass of tedious clerical and checking work in minutes, after hours of hard research by The Football League and computer staffs to feed it the right information, the right background and the right questions.

It is The Football League who are responsible for the final fixture lists, so it is pointless blaming Computer KDF9 if you find something in the fixtures which is open to question.

But before you criticise ... think on this: if man and machine working together for over six months can't improve on the 1,000 impossible conundrums, which make up a season's League fixtures, what makes you think you could do any better?

As a computer scientist brought in to cut irritations and problems to the minimum I will tell you frankly ... it is just not possible for any better results from what is nothing but a gigantic cross-word puzzle of problems.

They're all in the Game

Footballers, their coaches and their managers are sometimes somewhat scathing about what they describe as 'the game's hangers-on'.

They tend to get irritated by the numbers of people involved in football administration, by the people who make a living on its fringe.

But the highly-sophisticated modern game, if we can apply an analogy, is like the Army . . . to put one player on the field' requires nine back-stage personnel. Without the 'Unknown Soldiers' the game would grind to a halt.

Secretaries, gatemen, electricians, ground staff, kit manufacturers, painters, policemen, bus drivers, railway personnel, bar tenders, caterers, stewards, printers, journalists . . . the list is endless. And where would the football club be without them?

Football League club staffs reflect the trend. Arsenal, for instance, employ an architect on a part-time basis, Leeds United call on the services of a Methodist Minister for welfare work among their players, Everton and many others employ highly-skilled Commercial Managers to exploit their sales potential, Stoke City pay for visits to their dressing room by a skilled hairdresser, Halifax Town have a master plumber on the Board.

They are only a few of many possible examples, but they serve to illustrate the vast back-room army of people who these days keep a League club ticking over.

What good would even the best of players, the best of teams be, without the network of communicators . . . local and national sports writers, television and radio technicians and the film men, who project results, pictures, stories, personalities, and statistics of the game across to you.

In the following pages we examine the work of behind-the-scenes personnel at the clubs, and around the clubs . . . the people in the factories who make soccer kit and equipment . . . the people who help project the game . . . the countless people who make League football possible, whose contributions enable the star footballers to entertain millions week in and week out.

The first group of people are directly concerned with the club –

The Rev. John Jackson – Parson at Leeds United.

A physiotherapist at work at Stoke City.

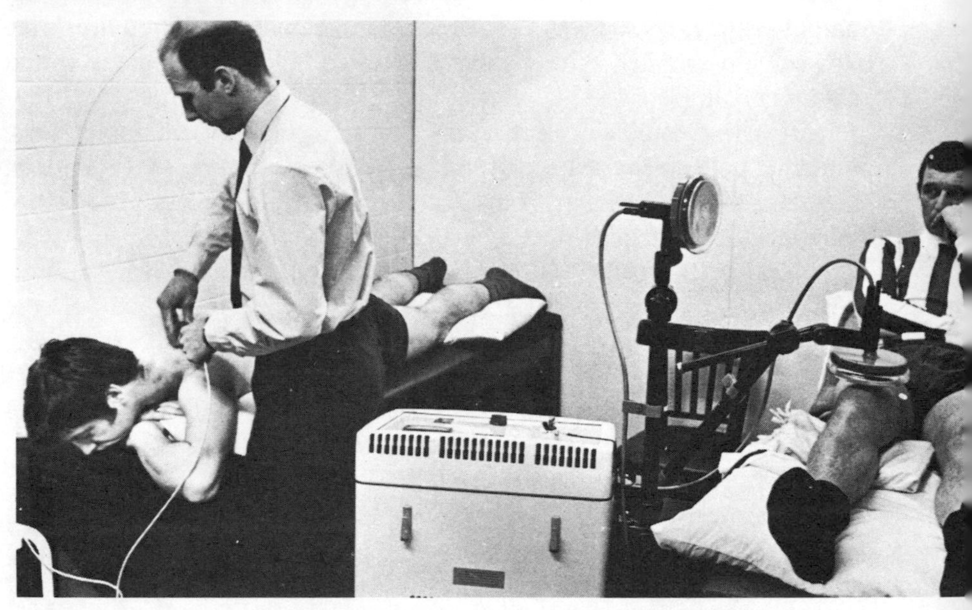

involved with the fitness of players, the treatment of injuries, the care and maintenance of the ground and administration.

The Trainer, once unkindly tagged the 'bucket and sponge' expert undertakes a far more sophisticated role than his predecessor did. He is responsible for the treatment of injuries during a game.

He carries a variety of accessories in his equipment. In a track suit pocket are: tie-ups for stockings, spare laces, aeromatic ammonia capsules, scissors, bayolin, or algipan for massage, a towel and a sponge.

Carried in a holdall are: bandages, a roll of sticky tape, lint, cotton wool, spare studs and a spanner to fit them, spare shorts, and extra goalkeeper's shirt, laces . . . and yet more elastic bandage.

The Physiotherapist's duties are an extension of the trainer's, in the treatment and medical rooms. He has highly technical and expensive equipment under his control and will have undergone an extensive grounding in physiology and anatomy. Many of the game's outstanding managers did part of their apprenticeship in medical rooms where the treatment may be complex but the object is basic – to minimise the effects of injury so that players are able to return to training as quickly as possible.

The Groundsman's main task is the preparation of the playing surface. He supervises mowing, rolling, seeding and general maintenance of the pitch and the terraces. At less affluent clubs his jobs will also include other roles – painter, carpenter or the odd-job man.

The Secretary is the key figure in the club's administration. He is responsible for everything outside the playing sphere, from the paying of salaries and wages to arranging ticket distribution. The secretary must be familiar with the Rules of the Football Association, the Regulations of The Football League and the intricacies of Company Law (all but Nottingham Forest are Limited Companies), as he is the man responsible by Law for the proper functioning of the Company.

He will be directly involved with every piece of off-the-field organisation including, for example, liaison with the police on such matters as crowd control and parking facilities at the ground.

In addition to more routine clerical duties, a secretary is responsible for catering arrangements on the ground and the production of the club programme. These specialist tasks are often controlled by people experienced in the two fields, but a club secretary must ensure that the service provided to spectators is as efficient as possible.

The Police used inside a ground are paid for by the club at an hourly rate, which differs throughout the country. The total cost can exceed £200 for a First Division game. The number used depends on the anticipated attendance and the degree of difficulty expected in crowd control. Clubs are not financially responsible for police used outside the grounds on crowd or traffic control.

Catering Staffs. Many clubs employ catering organisations to promote the sales of snacks and refreshments. At an average First Division match for example, caterers dispense nearly 10,000 cups of tea. 4,500 pies and 7,000 bottles of beer, at a rate of 700 items a minute.

Programme production is often in the charge of a trained journalist, although at smaller clubs the secretary is still personally responsible for the content and production of the programme.

Match Postponements. The financial problems of late postponements – to both clubs and supporters – prompted The League to introduce an Early Warning System two years ago. The match referee or a local League official is called in, often the day before the game, to inspect doubtful ground conditions and assess whether the fixture should be postponed. A late postponement means that many hours of work and money are wasted as part-time staff who have arrived at the ground have to be paid, and perishable food and drinks often have to be thrown away. Expenses have to be paid to the visiting team who, like the supporters, have wasted a journey.

Cleaning Staff. After every game, grounds are littered with rubbish of all kinds – plastic tea beakers, bottles, cigarette packets, old newspapers, sandwich and chocolate wrappers and so on. Clearing the terraces is a major operation often taking several days' work by the ground staff. Industrial cleaning equipment is unsatisfactory on most terraces and in many stands so the work remains mainly a manual operation.

The First Aid Personnel play a vital role in the modern soccer drama. Every ground provides first aid facilities of some nature for spectators, usually in the form of St John Ambulance or Red Cross attendants.

Brisk business at a League Club shop.

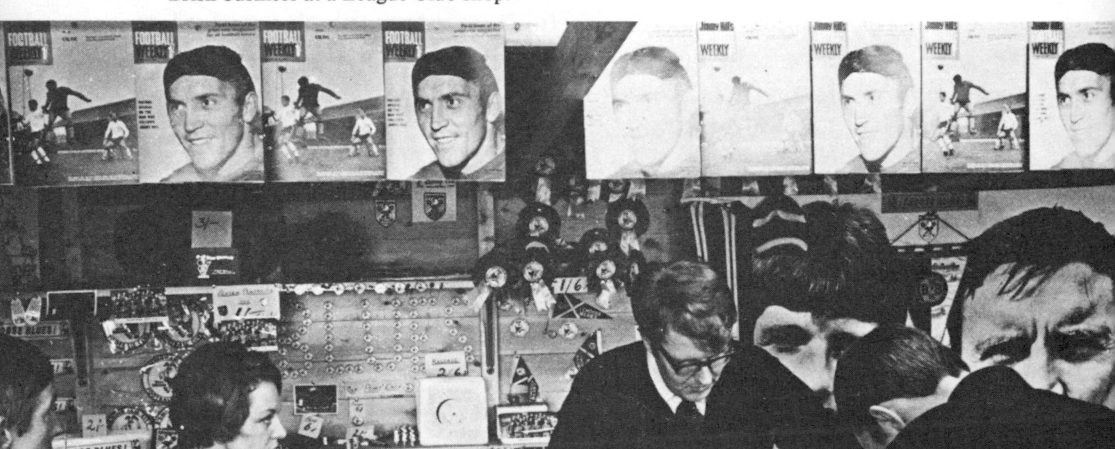

Most casualties among the crowd are fainting cases but more serious accidents do occur and many clubs now provide first-class medical rooms.

The Referee is responsible for the control of the game according to The Laws. His equipment covers eight essential items: a football, a wrist watch, a stop watch, a coin for tossing up at the start, a notebook in which he records the names of any players disciplined and relevant match details, two pencils, a whistle and a spare whistle.

The graduation of a referee from local parks to full League status is a complex procedure but basically it involves three stages:

1. Attendance at a referee's course run by County Associations and the sitting of the Class Three Examination.

2. Experience in minor football and the passing of the Class Two Examination.

3. Further experience in junior football before attempting the Class One Examination.

After surmounting these stages, a referee has to progress through supplementary Feeder and Contributory leagues before he attains the necesssary standard to be considered for promotion on to The Football League list. Even then he is closely watched and assessed by clubs and former League match officials who see that the high standard is maintained.

Press Photographers may be working for evening newspapers, in which case the photographs taken during an afternoon are rushed back to the local office dark room for developing and processing to appear in the football paper only minutes after the game ends.

A national newspaper photographer does not normally work to such a tight schedule on Saturday afternoons but is often hard-pressed at evening games.

At more important matches mobile transmitting stations are positioned near to the ground and the photographs wired direct to the newspaper offices.

Some grounds have installed special floodlights fitted with mercury-iodide lamps to improve the light quality for photography at evening matches – evidence of the way floodlighting is now accepted in the modern game.

Floodlights. It was at their annual meeting in June 1958 that The League clubs agreed to allow floodlighting to be used, provided the lights reached an approved standard. The angle of light has to be

A club official operates a computer used to count the spectators.

carefully controlled to ensure there is no danger of dazzling the players. Adequate lighting must also be provided to cover entrances.

Club-Fan Communication. Rapid strides have been made by clubs in the field of communication with the supporters. More informative programmes, better facilities and a general improvement in all-round amenities point the way ahead. The relaying of crowd messages by elaborate methods is an example of the importance which clubs give to this facet of their relationship with the public.

Sheffield Wednesday's Hillsborough ground, among the best appointed in Europe, boasts a magnificent electronically controlled scoreboard on which injury details, scorers and substitutions, and S.O.S. messages, can be flashed as soon as they are known. A similar electronic 'notice board' has been installed at Wembley Stadium, operated by one man sitting by a keyboard in the Stadium's Press Gallery.

Most clubs rely on the tannoy system to broadcast messages to crowds, in many instances competing against a background of chanting and widespread noise. Messages are often urgent and some clubs still fall back on to a chalked message on a blackboard carried round the perimeter by a member of the staff.

Electronic Counters. Counting spectators entering the ground through turnstiles once posed special problems for clubs, but a computer-type adding machine is now used on all the larger grounds. It automatically registers when an individual passes through the turnstile enabling club officials to ascertain exactly how many spectators are in any part of the ground at a given time, and which sections are near to being filled. People outside the stadium can thus be re-directed into less-populated parts of the ground and admittance to crowded sections stopped.

Football Manufacture. The manufacture of a football is still an example of the craftsman's art. No machine has yet been invented which replaces the individual skill required to turn a flat piece of leather into a round ball.

It takes almost three hours to produce one football casing, and at the Slazenger factory in Wakefield, Yorkshire, 1,000,000 square feet of leather is used every year to make sport goods – 80 per cent for the production of footballs.

Making Goal Posts. The quality of patience is also a pre-requisite for the manufacture of goal posts and cross bars. A Nottingham firm, Standard Goals Ltd, have been responsible for these for more than half a century. Although some automation has been introduced into the production, a high degree of individual craft from the joiner is still essential. A set of posts takes about a week to produce and the cost, including ground sockets, is almost £100. The firm also play a part in the country's export drive – they supply goal frames to Italy, South Africa, the Middle East and the West Indies.

The Communicators. Football's mass appeal is reflected by saturation coverage afforded it by the communications industry – press, radio and

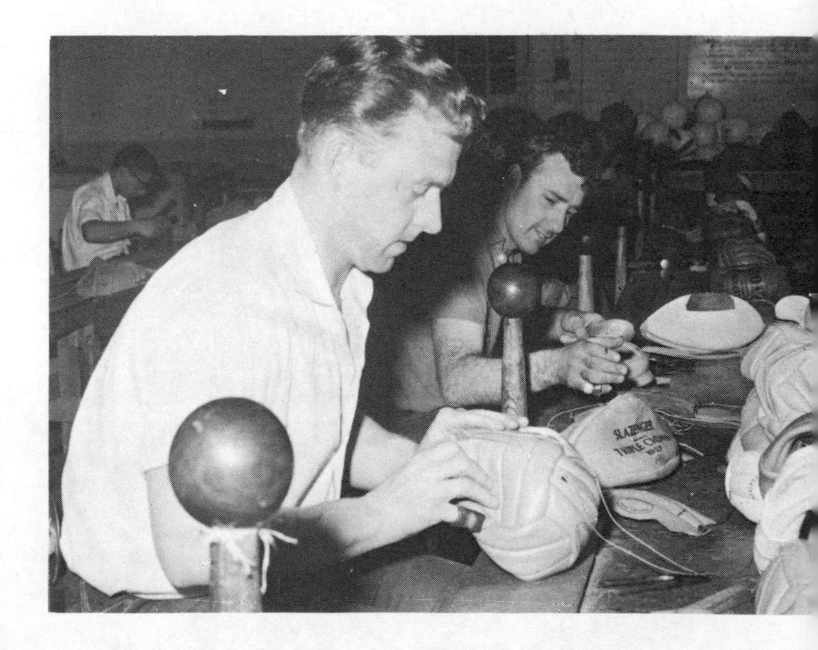

Making Football casing at the Slazengers factory in Wakefield, Yorks.

television. An increasing number of clubs determined to carve out their own image, have taken journalists on their staffs as public relations officers.

Public relations is still comparatively new in football but the success it has achieved at clubs like Coventry City, and indeed the establishment of a public relations department within The League organisation, shows it is a fast developing facet of the football industry.

Club public relations officers are responsible for the club image while Commercial Managers are the latest newcomers to the scene, controlling pools associations, development funds and club shops which provide vital sources of income for so many clubs.

Do you see, now, why we claim it takes at least nine people to put one footballer on the park. It is probably a conservative figure, at that.

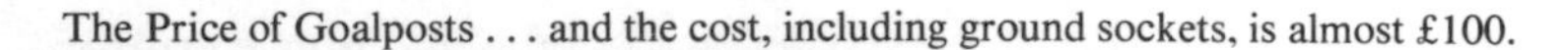

The Price of Goalposts . . . and the cost, including ground sockets, is almost £100.

How the League Outwitted the Football Alliance

WALTER PILKINGTON

The story of the Football League is a true romance of sport. It started with this name in humble fashion eighty-two years ago, so called because there was no other organisation of its kind. For this reason hints and suggestions about re-titling it The English League were always proudly rejected.

The League began with twelve clubs, six from Lancashire, six from the Midlands. By 1950, it had grown to ninety-two. Far-sighted planners would like to see its strength reach a hundred - five Divisions with twenty Clubs each. It is envied in every foreign country as the strongest and best organised football competition in the world. It set a widely copied pattern by pioneering the now universal points system, promotion and relegation, and the transfer of registered players. Ten years ago it promoted its own Cup competition. This much criticised venture vindicated the vision which created it by eventually providing a showpiece Wembley Final, assured of a 100,000 crowd. Small at the start, the gates at these Cup-ties gradually increased, then doubled to easily pass the two-million mark.

In the first season of the League 5,000 was a fair gate at large matches. By 1939 the spectator aggregate was verging on 28,000,000 a season. A peak total of 41,271,424 was reached in the third season of the post-war boom period. Interest then waned and the ensuing slump reduced the attendance to 27,206,596 in 1965–6. The subsequent revival has pushed the figures up again past 30,000,000.

The first £1,000 transfer, in 1905 - Alf Common, from Sunderland to Middlesbrough - was a sensation (the top fee ten years earlier was £250). This upward spiral has never stopped. Arsenal put the record into five figures in 1928 by paying £10,890 to Bolton for David Jack. By 1960 the highest fee had become £55,000 and six years later, £100,000 was paid three times.

At a rational estimate the value of players registered by First Division clubs is £20,000,000 at current rates.

Such is the vast expansion of The League and its interests. It is a development not for one moment dreamed of when the first president,

Mr William McGregor of Aston Villa, soon after professionalism had been legalised, wrote his historic letter to five clubs - Aston Villa, Blackburn Rovers, Bolton Wanderers, Preston North End, and West Bromwich Albion - inviting them to consider ways and means of forming a competition. His concern was that of getting matches properly organised and making them pay more.

The name he suggested was Association Football Union, to be run by a representative from each of ten or twelve prominent clubs. The problem was that of arranging and fulfilling friendly matches without cup-tie interference. On the evening of the 1888 Football Association Cup Final, at a conference at Anderton's Hotel, Fleet Street, Mr McGregor's ideas were approved and The Football League came into being with twelve clubs - the five mentioned, plus Accrington, Burnley, Derby County, Everton, Notts County, Stoke and Wolverhampton Wanderers. Firm fixture lists and punctual starts were insisted upon from the beginning.

The basic essential was that the clubs should support each other and bind themselves to carry out arrangements in the strictest sense. It proved to be a fundamental factor in the success achieved after the anticipated teething troubles. At first, points from wins and draws decided League positions. In the second season goal average was introduced and administration was put in the hands of a Management Committee. The four clubs at the bottom of the League had to retire, but were eligible for re-election. Stoke were refused this vote of confidence after two seasons (though they came back a year later) and were replaced by Sunderland, who stayed in the premier Division for a record fifty-seven seasons.

Inevitably the League system was copied and a strong rival body, known as the Football Alliance, was formed. The League decided that the best way to beat their rivals was to bring these clubs into the League network, hence the introduction in 1892 of a Second Division and the enlargement of the original group to sixteen clubs. The League's growth since the opening season is shown by the following table:

Period	*Seasons*	*Divisions and clubs*				*Total*
		1	2	3S	3N	
1888–91	3	12				12
1891–92	1	14				14
1892–93	1	16	12			28

FOOTBALL LEAGUE MANAGEMENT COMMITTEE 1969–70
Back left to right – A. Hardaker (secretary), F. Would (Grimsby), M. Glicksten (Charlton A.), R. Lord (Burnley), L. Edwards (Manchester United). *Front* – D. Wiseman (Birmingham City), W. Taylor (Newcastle United), L. T. Shipman (President) (Leicester City), S. Bolton (Leeds United), S. Collings (Sunderland).

Period	*Seasons*	*Divisions and clubs*				*Total*
		1	2	3S	3N	
1893–94	1	16	15			31
1894–98	4	16	16			32
1898–05	7	18	18			36
1905–15	10	20	20			40
1919–20	1	22	22			44
1920–21	1	22	22	22		66
1921–23	2	22	22	22	20	86
1923–50	20	22	22	22	22	88
1950–70	20	22	22	24x	24o	92
	71					

x – Div 3 o – Div 4

The formation of Division Two, as was expected, brought about the dissolution of The Football Alliance. It was good strategy and it enabled The League to go from strength to strength. Apart from one season, when Tottenham Hotspur won the Football Association Cup in 1901 as Southern Leaguers, the trophy has gone to a League club every year since 'Father' McGregor started bringing them under one banner in 1888. The only real challenge to The League's growing supremacy and prestige before World War I came from The Southern League. It was gradually whittled away as Bristol City, Chelsea, Clapton Orient, Fulham, and Tottenham Hotspur followed Woolwich Arsenal (elected 1893) into The Football League.

The conflict point was reached in 1919 with West Ham United's elevation to The League. As a result the Southern League terminated an agreement concerning the registration and transfer of players. But the problem was resolved by absorption. First Division Southern League clubs applied in 1920 to be taken into League membership as a Third Division, and it was agreed to accept them as associate members with no say in League management. As one result of this expansion, The League became lop-sided geographically and it was decided the following year to restore the balance by adding a Northern Section to Division Three.

Once again, shrewd government had kept The League on a foundation which was becoming more secure. Inevitably, however, mistakes were made in the early years. One was the selfish promotion-by-test-matches insisted upon by First Division clubs. On two or three occasions this farcical system denied Second Division clubs their due.

It all came to a head in 1898. Stoke and Burnley then realised that if each got a point from their final test match the one would not be relegated and the other would gain promotion. What looked suspiciously like an 'arrangement' resulted in the overdue abolition of the system and a further expansion of The League.

When the next increase of clubs – to twenty in each Division – was agreed to in 1905 it was proposed that three clubs instead of two should go up and down. The motion failed however.

Whether four-up, four-down will ever become the general practice remains as much a problem as it was fifty years ago when West Bromwich Albion were advocating it. The First Division clubs seem as likely as ever to abide by their long supported motto: Keep your numbers select!

The Communicators

Football is the greatest team sport in the world ... with the largest audience. More than 150 countries regard soccer as the national game.

But where would it be without The Communicators – that vast army of dedicated television, radio and newspaper reporters and analysts who flash the football news, views and controversies round town, city, country, world?

What makes them tick? What does their work demand of them? Here we give you just four examples from and about men who are proud to call themselves, each in his own sphere, The Communicators.

A National Newspaper Sports Editor

FRANK NICKLIN (*Sports Editor, The Sun*)

Some people will take a lot of convincing about this, but I swear it's true. We sports editors DO read your letters, and we DO take them seriously. Even though we don't always act on them.

I am thinking now of the two commonest of all. Believe me, if I had a pound note for every one of these letters I have received, I would have retired from this newspaper rat-race years ago!

LETTER No 1, usually signed 'Disgusted' goes like this: 'I read Charlie Bloggin's report on the Oxshott *v.* Bagshot match and I am convinced we were not watching the same game, etc, etc. Sack him!'

LETTER No 2, again from 'Disgusted' but this time written on a sugar bag, reads: 'You call Templegate a tipster? He couldn't tip a billiard cue, etc, etc. Sack him!'

Needless to say, Charlie Bloggins and Templegate are still working. Because the sports editor has been around long enough to appreciate that no two people see a football match or a horse race through the same pair of eyes. He knows his writers have graduated in a hard, professional school of journalism; that the standards are high, the competition is tough, and the pressure is on all the time; that for every printed story there may be a dozen that are unprintable; that there is a high moral code among these writers for accuracy and integrity.

He is conscious, above all, of the constant race against the clock. Always an edition to make, a train to be caught, a new reader to win. The greatest story in the world is useless if it is too late for the edition. For time is the master. On time means on sale.

That is why the sports editor must take overall responsibility for advance planning and the smooth running of the operation on the day. There can be no allowance for trial and error. It must be right first time.

One of the growing problems in recent years has been created by the vast increase of midweek floodlit football, not only at home but at European and international level.

Almost every week brings a big Continental fixture; often the kick-off is eight, nine or even ten o'clock, and that can play hell with ulcers – the chief sub-editor's, the circulation manager's and the poor, suffering sports editor's. Just try convincing the driver of the 10.20 that Newcastle didn't get the equaliser until the last minute of extra time and that he really should delay his departure while we rush off the glad news for Tyneside fans!

The role of the sports editor, particularly on a national newspaper, has gradually changed over the years. At one time he was the envy of the profession, covering all the big football and boxing matches often getting the 'plum' jobs and the more desirable foreign trips. Nowadays, the general tendency is to have an 'inside' man in charge. He works much closer to the printing and publishing sections; he attends daily editorial conferences in which sport plays an ever-increasing part; he spends a lot of time planning trans-Continental trips for other members of his staff. And believe me, that's the bit that really hurts!

As the size of national newspapers grows, so does the breadth of sports coverage. In the last year or two, competition has been sharper and, as sports editor of *The Sun* since it took on a new shape in

FRANK NICKLIN (Left)
Sun Sports Editor Frank Nicklin on the "stone" preparing an early page for Press. Later on the Composing room will be packed with people.

BBC RADIO (Right) The Sports team
Back row: Dick Scales, Liz Cooke, Jeremy Allerton, Godfrey Dixie, Simon Reed, John Motson. *Front row:* Peter Jones, Geoff Thomas, Angus Mackay, Bryon Butler, Emily McMahon, Margaret Mager, Bob Burrows.

November 1969, I have become personally involved in what Fleet Street has called 'The Battle of The Tabloids'. At such times, the pressure on the nervous system can be pretty shattering. The hours are longer, the moments of relaxation fewer and briefer. But the reward of an increasing circulation can have an exhilarating effect on a good sports team.

Reporting Football in the BBC

BRYON BUTLER (*BBC Football Correspondent*)

It was, you may think, a surprising answer. A seven-year-old boy, asked whether he preferred television or radio, replied: 'Radio – because the pictures are better.'

Imagination is the one thing radio demands from its audience and, given this, it stands immediately as a medium with something to offer that neither television nor the newspaper can match. A radio voice cannot be seen or re-read but where there is imagination or, if you like, participation, it has, perhaps, most of all to offer.

I must be careful because I have a responsibility to television as well as radio, and this after more than 15 years as a newspaperman; but at a time when radio has been busy *making* news, with its recent reorganisation, it is also right to emphasise its unparalleled strength as a medium for *reporting* news. This includes sports news and, more particularly, football news.

Let us take, for example, the longest running sports programme of them all, 'Sports Report' which can be heard on Radio Two every Saturday during the football season and which has been on the road now for 22 years. It starts at five o'clock and, while grounds are still emptying, it provides the full classified results, on-the-spot reports on eight of the day's main matches, interviews with managers and players

in the news, a round-up of other games and a run-down of the day's vital statistics (crowds, League positions, leading goal-scorers, etc).

It provides all this well before the Pinks, Buffs and Green 'Uns are on the streets, more than 12 hours before the Sunday papers have a go, and nearly two days before the nationals take their turn on Monday.

The daily coverage of sport is also sharp, comprehensive – and first. It begins with Morning Sportsdesk in the 'Today' programme (Radio Four, 7 and 8 a.m.). It continues with Sportsdesk (Radio Two, 6.50 p.m.) which extends the coverage of the evenings and anticipates the next morning's sports pages. It finishes with Late Night Extra Sportsdesk (Radio One and Two, 10.15 p.m.) which is always first with the results and details of evening matches. It is quite a line-up.

Radio can dispense news immediately. It does not require the technical paraphernalia of television, nor does it need the time-consuming, conveyor belt treatment that every newspaper story needs.

Radio is also the one and only regular source of live football coverage. It provides on Radio Two a commentary on a major League or Cup match every Saturday and on many of the season's big midweek games.

The audience figures are good – and growing – which suggests there are a lot of people who, given the chance, like to use their imagination.

Soccer As the Provincial Newspaperman Sees It

TONY PRITCHETT (*Sports Writer, Sheffield Star*)

Some years ago, I sat over dinner with a soccer manager and his chairman. And I listened with embarrassment as the manager discussed what he was going to do with his team next season . . . embarrassment because I knew, and the chairman knew that I knew, the manager wouldn't be with the club much longer. Someone else was lined up to take over.

I recount this story to illustrate how close to a club the provincial reporter can become and how difficult it is to walk the tightrope of discretion.

Many provincial papers employ the one-man-per-club system in which one member of their sports staff is made entirely responsible for news gathering. This so-close relationship frequently leads to the discovery of off-the-record news items or the hearing of conversations which could make sensational headlines next day.

TONY PRITCHETT
Sheffield Star football correspondent whose main task is to cover the activities of Sheffield Wednesday. Formerly the Forest man at the Nottingham Evening Post.

The difficulty is in deciding what can legitimately be used without being accused of a breach of confidence and what must be kept quiet. Usually the reporter strikes up a good working relationship with the manager of his club. If he doesn't, well he doesn't get the stories anyway.

The trap in all this of course is to become nothing more than the mouthpiece of the club. There can be a danger that in return for the comfort and privilege of being 'one of the official party' on away games, a reporter can project merely those stories which put the team in a good light, and sit on all the others because somebody might not like it.

There is room in this area, surely, for a closer co-operation between club and paper. I often wonder why clubs don't make better use of the publicity medium that is open to them every day of the week.

In my view it should be possible for the name of the town's football club or clubs to appear on the sports pages of the local paper every single night. Many clubs pass up this opportunity because they simply do not recognise the value of the public relations side of their job.

Happily I feel this 'Keep the press at arm's length' attitude is dwindling. Coventry set a magnificent example. In Sheffield, Eric Taylor needs no one to tell him the value of the right kind of publicity – but there are still many clubs who miss out.

There needs to be tact employed particularly on the part of the reporter. The provincial man must maintain a respectable relationship with his local officials. If the Fleet Street writers upset a manager, so what? There are 91 more in The League to go at aren't there?

It must be a matter of give and take. After all, the men who run soccer know we want stories. At the same time we know there are some good stories they don't want to see in print. So long as there is nothing malicious, sarcastic or downright trouble-stirring in the papers, I reckon many managers realise that problems of transfers, contract difficulties etc, are part of the soccer scene, and are meat and drink to the public who pay their wages – as well as the reporter's.

It really is a tightrope. An exercise in discretion. The closer one works with fellow professionals the greater the hurt can be when a critical story is splashed all over the back page.

The pitfalls are always there. I know, I've fallen into a good few myself over the years.

Does Television Kid the Football Public?

Are the BBC and ITV leading the football public up the garden path? Are they breaking their necks to sell the game as they would soap powder? That is the verdict of some critics.

The Sunday Express has said: 'Neither is concerned with the real values of the game. They would have us believe there is no 'bad' in their world, that all (in football) is scintillating and terrific and marvellous'. Is that fair comment?

Another critic suggested: 'Perhaps the television people are afraid that if they tell the truth about some matches they have to televise, then The Football League will bring pressure to bear on them.' That most certainly is neither fair nor true.

Both TV Channels pay for the right to televise their recorded match reports which go out on Saturday nights and Sunday afternoons. They pay a total of nearly a quarter of a million pounds for the privilege.

Can anyone really expect them to edit a 45-minute recording of a 90-minute match to include the dull bits ... when they are seeking entertainment for their viewers?

ITV's Assistant Director of Sport, Gerry Loftus, told us: 'We are putting entertainment on to our screens, and our editors and producers must look for that entertainment when they are cutting a match down to the recording time limits.

'Do critics really expect us to produce the dullest 45 minutes we can find? Our viewers certainly don't.'

We do think that is fair comment. The Football League puts no pressure on either channel about the way they present matches ... except that they expect balanced comment on match incidents. The way the companies edit the recording is up to them.

Television camera focused on an important game . . . a normal sight now on League grounds.

Bryan Cowgill, the BBC Head of Outside Broadcasts, told us: 'Football goes on the screens because it is an entertainment. Our contracts with The League allow us to present only 45 minutes of a game, and on film at that. If we did not present the most exciting excerpts of that game then we would not be playing fair with our viewers. That is sound commonsense.'

We agree.

But why does neither channel attempt to diagnose the dull spots for the sake of balance?

Says Mr Cowgill: 'We screen our games within five hours or so of the finish. It needs all that time, and more, to edit the highlights without analysing the low lights. It is impossible.

'Nevertheless when we are cutting we must always attempt to keep a balance between entertainment value and what actually happened.'

Says Mr Loftus: 'Even though we have a little more time, staff and technical difficulties in most regions make real analysis out of the question. But I think the game itself, good or bad, comes through.'

So do we.

As Mr Loftus says: 'I have been in the game for nearly 30 years as player, journalist, TV commentator and TV administrator. The game today is better than ever before, and those who dub it as dirtier than ever before can have very little knowledge of what went on before the war.'

We can only agree. Again.

We would add this: if there is anything wrong with the game as it is screened is it not perhaps a greater reflection on the players under review than the television channels?

Why Shouldn't Their Home Be Lytham?

TOM POMFRET (*Editor, Lytham St Annes Express*)

Lytham St Annes, its roots fed by the rich greens and fairways of golfing country, is the adopted home of The Football League.

Born out of the urban councils of Lytham and St Annes in 1922, it grew up as a dormitory town for Manchester and industrial Lancashire. Cotton and industrial moguls settled on the banks of the River Ribble and stately homes proliferated.

According to some Press reports, 'Princes of Cotton' found peace which was only disturbed by the development of the combustion engine. Indeed, at one time street corners sprouted signs, 'char-a-bancs prohibited', a ban which convinced many Blackpool business people that their neighbours along the Fylde coast had 'got a little above their station!'

The town was said to be the home of peppery colonels with monocles and white-haired old ladies concentrating industriously on their clicking knitting needles.

This, of course, was a caricature of the real Lytham St Annes. After the war, when the civil service became a growth industry in the town, it faded almost completely. In 1956 Ernie Premium Bond was born at St Annes. Three years later, in 1959, The Football League moved its headquarters from Preston to St Annes.

Today, Ernie, the Football League and the Royal Lytham St Annes Golf Club, where both Ryder Cup and Open golf championship battles have been fought, are the town's three publicity aces.

Four golf courses and international sand yachting dominate the summer holiday sporting scene. Scots holidaymakers, in particular, flock to the town to mix golf with a family holiday. The League's arrival in 1959 brought the town added publicity. It was welcome and needed. Just how needed it was is best illustrated by one or two early national newspaper reports of League meetings 'at its Blackpool headquarters'. Dear, dear!

The League has now lived a decade in the town. Yet, from time to time, suggestions are made that geographically, and for other obscure reasons, it is sited in the wrong place. Why? After all, Blackpool airport is inside the town's boundaries. London is only four hours away by rail, the M6 has brought the Midlands within two-and-half to three hours of Lytham St Annes.

League soccer was born in the North and Midlands. For more than half a century its administration thrived at Preston, only 15 miles from Lytham St Annes. By the time it arrived here it had long held the rightful claim to have established the finest football competition in the world.

A move into modern and well-equipped new offices in Clifton-drive South, only 15 miles from Preston, has not put the clock back. Today it is still on the fringe of the most successful and affluent belt of soccer clubs in Britain.

Lancashire, and Lytham St Annes in particular, are delighted to have The Football League in their midst. The FA headquarters are in London. The county's football fans have to trek to London for the FA Cup and League Cup Finals, and for most of the big international matches.

A League headquarters in the North, near to its birthplace, seems logical to northern soccer fans. Long may it thrive in the county where its roots are deep.

Football League Headquarters at Lytham St. Annes.

Statistics

League Leaders

Founder and first Chairman of The Football League, *Mr William McGregor*. He conceived the idea of the world's first Association Football League. Chairman from the foundation in 1888 to 1892.

PRESIDENTS

Mr William McGregor, of Birmingham - 1892–4

Mr J. J. Bentley, of Bolton - 1894–1910

Held office during the difficult years of growth and stabilisation.

Mr John McKenna, of Liverpool - 1910–36

A disciplinarian whose bark was worse than his bite, kept firm control and his 26 years in the chair was the longest-ever Presidential control.

Mr Charles E. Sutcliffe, of Rawtenstall - 1936–9

A solicitor he had been Mr McKenna's right-hand man and his brief reign was a stern one. During his 51 years' association with The League he had a hand in much vital legislation a great deal of which lives on.

Mr W. C. Cuff, of Liverpool - 1939–49

The leader during the difficult war and post-war years.

Mr Arthur Drewry, C.B.E., of Grimsby 1949–55

Presided over the launching of the Players' Provident Fund. Resigned to take over as Chairman of The Football Association.

Mr A. H. Oakley, of Wolverhampton - 1955–57

Concluded a long period of service as referee and club director by taking over as President.

Sir Joseph Richards, of Barnsley - 1957–66

Held office during changing times, amid new and pressing problems. These included the removal of the players' maximum wage, the problem of handling television in the best interests of the game, the introduction of Substitutes, negotiating Pools payments for the copyright of fixtures, the introduction of The League Cup competition and the foundation of Football League Review and a Public

Relations Department within The League. A memorable record from a man who was deservedly Knighted for his services to the game.

Mr Leonard Shipman, M.B.E, of Leicester – 1966–

Has carried on where Sir Joseph left off. Engaged in continuing legislation with the P.F.A. for mutual benefit he has also seen the introduction of sponsorship with the Watney Mann Cup competition and the Ford Sporting League. A great deal of new money is coming into the game and his aim is to supply a pattern of acceptable sponsorship which can be emulated by sporting bodies all over the world.

LEAGUE SECRETARIES

During the 82 years of its existence The Football League has been served by only four Secretaries all of whom have left an indelible mark on the game:

Mr H. Locket *1888–1902* *Mr Fred Howarth* *1933–57*
Mr Tom Charnley *1902–33* *Mr Alan Hardaker* *1957–*

CLUB PLACINGS THROUGH THE YEARS

This chart gives at-a-glance details of the length of time each club in present membership of The League has spent in each of the divisions as well as the year in which it was admitted to The Football League.

Please note that clubs who have changed their names are recorded under their present name although their records under old titles are included. But where new clubs have replaced old clubs in the same place (e.g. Leeds United replaced the expunged Leeds City) only the record of the new club is shown.

CLUB	ELECTED	DIVISION						TOTAL SEASONS IN LEAGUE
		1	2	3S	3N	3	4	
Aldershot	1932			19			12	31
Arsenal	1893	53	13					66
Aston Villa	1888	65	6					71
Barnsley	1898		45		5	8	3	61
Barrow	1921				30	3	9	42

CLUB	ELECTED	DIVISION						TOTAL SEASONS IN LEAGUE
		1	2	3S	3N	3	4	
Birmingham C	1892	38	29					67
Blackburn	1888	54	17					71
Blackpool	1896	26	36					62
Bolton Wan	1888	58	13					71
Bournemth & B	1923			28			12	40
Bradford C.	1903	10	18		16	4	8	56
Bradford	1908	3	22		14	2	10	51
Brentford	1920	5	9	17		7	5	43
Brighton & H	1920		4	31		6	2	43
Bristol City	1901	5	28	20		5		58
Bristol Rov	1920		9	26		8		43
Burnley	1888	47	24					71
Bury	1894	17	37		6	5		65
Cardiff City	1920	15	19	9				43
Carlisle U	1928		5		23	2	5	35
Charlton	1921	14	18	10				42
Chelsea	1905	43	11					54
Chester	1931				20		12	32
Chesterfield	1899		20		20	3	9	52
Colchester	1950			8		8	4	20
Coventry City	1919	3	18	16	1	5	1	44
Crewe Alex	1892		4		30	2	10	46
Crystal Pal	1920	1	9	27		3	3	43
Darlington	1921		2		28	1	11	42
Derby Co	1888	44	25		2			71
Doncaster R	1901		14		17	3	9	43
Everton	1888	67	4					71
Exeter City	1921			31		2	10	43
Fulham	1907	12	35	4		1		52
Gillingham	1920			26		6	6	38
Grimsby Town	1892	12	34	1	10	7	2	66
Halifax Town	1921				30	6	6	42
Hartlepool	1921				30	1	11	42
Hudsfld Town	1910	28	21					49
Hull City	1905		36		11	7		54
Ipswich Town	1938	5	9	11				25
Leeds United	1920	24	19					43

CLUB	ELECTED	DIVISION						TOTAL SEASONS IN LEAGUE
		1	2	3S	3N	3	4	
Leicester City	1894	26	39					65
Lincoln City	1892		34		21	1	8	64
Liverpool	1893	55	11					66
Luton Town	1897	5	17	17		4	3	46
Manchester C	1892	50	17					67
Manchester U	1892	46	21					67
Mansfield T	1931			4	16	9	3	32
Middlesbrough	1899	37	22			1		60
Millwall	1920		13	22		3	5	43
Newcastle	1893	50	16					66
Newport C	1920		1	29		4	8	42
Northampton	1920	1	3	31		4	4	43
Norwich C	1920		15	26		2		43
Notts Co	1888	26	24	9		5	7	71
Nottingham F	1892	34	31	2				67
Oldham A	1907	9	16		15	6	6	52
Orient	1905	1	29	20		4		54
Oxford United	1962		2			3	3	8
Peterboro U	1960					7	3	10
Plymouth A	1920		26	14		3		43
Portsmouth	1920	25	13	4		1		43
Port Vale	1892		32	8	5	6	6	57
Preston N E	1888	46	25					71
Queen's Park R	1920	1	6	27		9		43
Reading	1920		5	26		12		43
Rochdale	1921				30	2	10	42
Rotherham U	1893		24		21	2		47
Scunthorpe U	1950		6		8	4	2	20
Sheffield U	1892	50	17					67
Sheffield Wed	1892	51	16					67
Shrewsbury T	1950			7	1	11	1	20
Southampton	1920	4	30	7		2		43
Southend U	1920			31		8	4	43
Southport	1921				30	3	9	42
Stockport Co	1900		21		25	4	8	58
Stoke City	1888	39	23		1			63
Sunderland	1890	63	6					69

Swansea C	1920		31	7		2	3	43
Swindon Town	1920		3	31		9		43
Torquay U	1927			24		6	6	36
Tottenham H	1908	36	15					51
Tranmere R	1921		1		29	6	6	42
Walsall	1896		7	19	11	8	2	47
Watford	1920		1	31		9	2	43
West Brom A	1888	55	16					71
West Ham U	1919	21	23					44
Wolverhampton	1888	47	23		1			71
Workington	1951				7	3	9	19
Wrexham	1921				30	4	8	42
York City	1929				22	2	10	34

Inter League Matches

FOOTBALL LGE V SCOTTISH LGE

Played 67. England won 36; Scotland 18; drawn 13

Year	Venue	E – S
1892	Bolton	2 – 2
1893	Glasgow	4 – 3
1894	Liverpool	1 – 1
1895	Glasgow	4 – 1
1896	Liverpool	5 – 1
1897	Glasgow	0 – 3
1898	Birmingham	1 – 2
1899	Glasgow	4 – 1
1900	London	2 – 2
1901	Glasgow	2 – 6
1902	Newcastle	6 – 3
1903	Glasgow	3 – 0
1904	Manchester	2 – 1
1905	Glasgow	3 – 2
1906	London	6 – 2
1907	Glasgow	0 – 0
1908	Birmingham	2 – 0
1909	Glasgow	1 – 3
1910	Blackburn	2 – 3
1911	Glasgow	1 – 1
1912	Middlesbrough	2 – 0
1913	Glasgow	1 – 4
1914	Burnley	2 – 3
1915	Glasgow	4 – 1
1916-7-8	Not played	
1919*	Birmingham	3 – 1
1919*	Glasgow	2 – 3
1920	Glasgow	4 – 0
1921	Highbury	1 – 0
1922	Glasgow	3 – 0
1923	Newcastle	2 – 1
1924	Glasgow	1 – 1
1925	Everton	4 – 3
1926	Glasgow	2 – 0
1927	Leicester	2 – 2
1928	Glasgow	6 – 2
1929	Birmingham	2 – 1
1930	Glasgow	1 – 2
1931	Tottenham	7 – 3
1932	Glasgow	3 – 4
1933	Manchester	0 – 3
1934	Glasgow	2 – 2
1935	Chelsea	2 – 1
1936	Glasgow	2 – 2
1937	Everton	2 – 0

1938	Glasgow	0 – 1	1959	Glasgow	1 – 1
1939	Wolverhampton	3 – 1	1960	Highbury	1 – 0
1940–	46 Not played		1961	Glasgow	2 – 3
1947	Glasgow	3 – 1	1962	Villa Park	3 – 4
1948	Newcastle	1 – 1	1963	no match	
1949	Glasgow	3 – 0	1964	Sunderland	2 – 2
1950	Middlesbrough	3 – 1	1965	Glasgow	2 – 2
1951	Glasgow	0 – 1	1966	Newcastle	1 – 3
1952	Sheffield	2 – 1	1967	Glasgow	3 – 0
1953	Glasgow	0 – 1	1968	Middlesbrough	2 – 0
1954	Chelsea	4 – 0	1969	Glasgow	3 – 1
1955	Glasgow	2 – 3	1970	Coventry	3 – 2
1956	Sheffield	4 – 2			——
1957	Glasgow	2 – 3			160–107
1958	Newcastle	4 – 1			

*'Victory' matches, not official and excluded from table.

FOOTBALL LGE V IRISH LGE

Played 60. England won 53; Ireland 3; Drawn 4.

		E – I			
1894	Belfast	4 – 2	1915	West Bromwich	2 – 1
1895	Not played		1916–7–8–9	Not played	
1896	Stoke	2 – 2	1920	Liverpool	2 – 2
1897	Belfast	2 – 0	1921	Not played	
1898	Manchester	8 – 1	1922	Belfast	1 – 0
1899	Belfast	5 – 1	1923	Bolton	5 – 1
1900	Bolton	3 – 1	1924	Belfast	9 – 2
1901	Belfast	4 – 2	1925	Belfast	5 – 0
1902	Woolwich	9 – 0	1926	Liverpool	5 – 1
1903	Belfast	3 – 2	1927	Belfast	6 – 1
1904	Bradford	2 – 1	1928	Newcastle	9 – 1
1905	Belfast	2 – 0	1929	Belfast	5 – 0
1906	Manchester	4 – 0	1930	Everton	5 – 2
1907	Belfast	6 – 0	1931	Belfast	2 – 2
1908	Sunderland	6 – 3	1932	Blackpool	4 – 0
1909	Belfast	5 – 0	1933	Belfast	5 – 2
1910	Oldham	8 – 1	1934	Preston	4 – 0
1911	Belfast	6 – 2	1935	Belfast	6 – 1
1912	Liverpool	4 – 0	1936	Blackpool	1 – 2
1913	Belfast	0 – 0	1937	Belfast	2 – 3
1914	Belfast	2 – 0	1938	Blackpool	3 – 0

1939	Belfast	8 – 2	1958	Belfast	4 – 2
1940-	1-2-3-4-5-6 Not played		1959	Liverpool	5 – 2
1947	Everton	4 – 2	1960	Belfast	5 – 0
1948	Belfast	4 – 3	1961	Blackpool	5 – 2
1949	Liverpool	5 – 1	1962	Belfast	6 – 1
1950	Belfast	3 – 1	1963	Norwich	3 – 1
1951	Blackpool	6 – 3	1964	no match	
1952	Belfast	9 – 0	1965	Belfast	4 – 0
1953	Wolverhampton	7 – 1	1966	no match	
1954	Belfast	5 – 0	1967	Plymouth	12 – 0
1955	Liverpool	4 – 2	1968	no match	
1956	Belfast	2 – 5	1969	Belfast	1 – 0
1957	Newcastle	3 – 2	1970	no match	
					270–68

FOOTBALL LGE V LGE OF IRELAND

Played 20. England won 17; L of I 1; Drawn 2.

		E – I			
			1959	Dublin	0 – 0
1947	Dublin	3 – 1	1960	Blackburn	2 – 0
1948	Preston	4 – 0	1961	Dublin	4 – 0
1949	Dublin	5 – 0	1962	Bristol	5 – 2
1950	Wolverhampton	7 – 0	1963	no match	
1951	Dublin	1 – 0	1964	Dublin	1 – 2
1952	Liverpool	9 – 1	1965	no match	
1953	Dublin	2 – 0	1966	Hull	5 – 0
1954	Manchester	9 – 1	1967	no match	
1955	Dublin	6 – 0	1968	Dublin	7 – 2
1956	Everton	5 – 1	1969	no match	
1957	Dublin	3 – 3	1970	Barnsley	3 – 0
1958	Leeds	3 – 1			
					84–14

FOOTBALL LGE V SOUTHERN LGE

Played 6. Won 4, Lost 1, Drawn 1, Goals 13–9.

		FL SL
1910	Chelsea	2 – 2
1911	Tottenham	2 – 3
1912	Stoke	2 – 1
		FL SL
1913	Manchester	2 – 1

1914	Millwall	3 - 1
1915	Highbury	2 - 1

FOOTBALL LGE V BELGIAN LGE

1968 Brussels — Fbl Lge 2 Belgium 2

FOOTBALL LGE V DANISH LGE

1953 Copenhagen — Fbl Lge 4 - 0

FOOTBALL LGE V ITALIAN LGE

Played 4, Won 1, Lost 3, Goals 5 - 9.

		FL IL
1961	Milan	2 - 4
1962	Old Trafford	0 - 2

		FL IL
1963	Highbury	3 - 2
1964	Milan	0 - 1

Football League Cup Finalists

	Winners		Runners-up	
1960–61	†Aston Villa	3	Rotherham United	2
1961–62	†Norwich City	4	Rochdale	0
1962–63	†Birmingham City	3	Aston Villa	1
1963–64	†Leicester City	4	Stoke City	3
1964–65	†Chelsea	3	Leicester City	2
1965–66	†West Bromwich Albion	5	West Ham United	3
1966–67	Queen's Park Rangers	3	West Bromwich Albion	2
1967–68	Leeds United	1	Arsenal	0
1968–69	*Swindon Town	3	Arsenal	1
1969–70	*Man City	2	West Bromwich Albion	1

†Result on aggregate, two legs.
*In extra time.

World Cup Winners

1966 (England)	—Champions	: ENGLAND
	2nd	: West Germany
	3rd	: Portugal
	4th	: U.S.S.R.
1970 (Mexico)	—Champions	: BRAZIL
	2nd	: Italy
	3rd	: West Germany
	4th	: Uruguay

1962 (Chile)	—Champions	:	BRAZIL
	2nd	:	Czechoslovakia
	3rd	:	Chile
	4th	:	Yugoslavia
1958 (Sweden)	—Champions	:	BRAZIL
	2nd	:	Sweden
	3rd	:	France
	4th	:	West Germany
1954 (Switzerland)	—Champions	:	WEST GERMANY
	2nd	:	Hungary
	3rd	:	Austria
	4th	:	Uruguay
1950 (Brazil)	—Champions	:	URUGUAY
	2nd	:	Brazil
	3rd	:	Sweden
	4th	:	Spain
1938 (France)	—Champions	:	ITALY
	2nd	:	Hungary
	3rd	:	Brazil
	4th	:	Sweden
1934 (Italy)	—Champions	:	ITALY
	2nd	:	Czechoslovakia
	3rd	:	Germany
	4th	:	Austria
1930 (Uruguay)	—Champions	:	URUGUAY
	2nd	:	Argentina
	3rd	:	U.S.A.
	4th	:	Yugoslavia

F.A. Cup Winners

(From when clubs subsequently in The League first appeared in the Final).

AT KENNINGTON OVAL

1881-2—Old Etonians beat Blackburn Rovers (1 - 0)
1882-3—Blackburn Olym. beat Old Etonians (2 - 1), after extra half-hour
1883-4—Blackburn Rovers beat Queen's Park (Glasgow) (2 - 1)

1884–5—Blackburn Rovers beat Queen's Park (Glasgow) (2 – 0)
1885–6—†‡Blackburn R. beat W. Brom. A. (2 – 0, after a draw 0 – 0)
1886–7—Aston Villa beat West Bromwich Albion (2 – 0)
1887–8—West Bromwich Albion beat Preston North End (2 – 1)
1888–9—Preston North End beat Wolverhampton Wanderers (3 – 0)
1889–90–Blackburn Rovers beat Sheffield Wednesday (6 – 1)
1890–1—Blackburn Rovers beat Notts County (3 – 1)
1891–2—West Bromwich Albion beat Aston Villa (3 – 0)

AT FALLOWFIELD, MANCHESTER

1892–3—Wolverhampton Wanderers beat Everton (1 – 0)

AT EVERTON

1893–4—Notts County beat Bolton Wanderers (4 – 1)

AT CRYSTAL PALACE

1894–5—Aston Villa beat West Bromwich Albion (1 – 0)
1895–6—Sheffield Wednesday beat Wolverhampton Wanderers (2 – 1)
1896–7—Aston Villa beat Everton (3 – 2)
1897–8—Nottingham Forest beat Derby County (3 – 1)
1898–9—Sheffield United beat Derby County (4 – 1)
1899–1900—Bury beat Southampton (4 – 0)
1900–1—‡‡Tottenham H. beat Sheffield U. (3 – 1, after a draw 2 – 2)
1901–2—Sheffield United beat Southampton (2 – 1 after a draw 1 – 1)
1902–3—Bury beat Derby County (6 – 0)
1903–4—Manchester City beat Bolton Wanderers (1 – 0)
1904–5—Aston Villa beat Newcastle United (2 – 0)
1905–6—Everton beat Newcastle United (1 – 0)
1906–7—Sheffield Wednesday beat Everton (2 – 1)
1907–8—Wolverhampton Wanderers beat Newcastle United (3 – 1)
1908–9—Manchester United beat Bristol City (1 – 0)
1909–10–**Newcastle United beat Barnsley (2 – 0, after a draw 1 – 1)
1910–11–*a*Bradford City beat Newcastle United (1 – 0, after a draw 0 – 0)
1911–12–*b*Barnsley beat West Bromwich Albion (1 – 0, after a draw 0 – 0 and an extra half-hour in the replay)
1912–13–Aston Villa beat Sunderland (1 – 0)
1913–14–Burnley beat Liverpool (1 – 0)

AT OLD TRAFFORD, MANCHESTER

1914–15–Sheffield United beat Chelsea (3 – 0)
1915–16, 1916–17, 1917–18, 1918–19—No competition

AT STAMFORD BRIDGE

1919–20–††Aston Villa beat Huddersfield Town (1 – 0)
1920–1—Tottenham Hotspur beat Wolverhampton Wanderers (1 – 0)
1921–2—Huddersfield Town beat Preston North End (1 – 0)

AT WEMBLEY STADIUM

1922–3—Bolton Wanderers beat West Ham United (2 – 0)
1923–4—Newcastle United beat Aston Villa (2 – 0)
1924–5—Sheffield United beat Cardiff City (1 – 0)
1925–6—Bolton Wanderers beat Manchester City (1 – 0)
1926–7—Cardiff City beat Arsenal (1 – 0)
1927–8—Blackburn Rovers beat Huddersfield Town (3 – 1)
1928–9—Bolton Wanderers beat Portsmouth (2 – 0)
1929–30–Arsenal beat Huddersfield Town (2 – 0)
1930–1—West Bromwich Albion beat Birmingham (2 – 1)
1931–2—Newcastle United beat Arsenal (2 – 1)
1932–3—Everton beat Manchester City (3 – 0)
1933–4—Manchester City beat Portsmouth (2 – 1)
1934–5—Sheffield Wednesday beat West Bromwich Albion (4 – 2)
1935–6—Arsenal beat Sheffield United (1 – 0)
1936–7—Sunderland beat Preston North End (3 – 1)
1937–8—††Preston North End beat Huddersfield Town (1 – 0)
1938–9—Portsmouth beat Wolverhampton Wanderers (4 – 1)
1939–45–Competition cancelled owing to war
1945–6—††Derby County beat Charlton Athletic (4 – 1)
1946–7—††Charlton Athletic beat Burnley (1 – 0)
1947–8—Manchester United beat Blackpool (4 – 2)
1948–9—Wolverhampton Wanderers beat Leicester City (3 – 1)
1949–50–Arsenal beat Liverpool (2 – 0)
1950–1—Newcastle United beat Blackpool (2 – 0)
1951–2—Newcastle United beat Arsenal (1 – 0)
1952–3—Blackpool beat Bolton Wanderers (4 – 3)
1953–4—West Bromwich Albion beat Preston north End (3 – 2)
1954–5—Newcastle United beat Manchester City (3 – 1)
1955–6—Manchester City beat Birmingham City (3 – 1)
1956–7—Aston Villa beat Manchester United (2 – 1)
1957–8—Bolton Wanderers beat Manchester United (2 – 0)
1958–9—Nottingham Forest beat Luton Town (2 – 1)
1959–60–Wolverhampton Wanderers beat Blackburn Rovers (3 – 0)
1960–1—Tottenham Hotspur beat Leicester City (2 – 0)
1961–2—Tottenham Hotspur beat Burnley (3 – 1)
1962–3—Manchester United beat Leicester City (3 – 1)

1963-4—West Ham United beat Preston North End (3 - 2)
1964-5—††Liverpool beat Leeds United (2 - 1)
1965-6—Everton beat Sheffield Wednesday (3 - 2)
1966-7—Tottenham Hotspur beat Chelsea (2 - 1)
1967-8—††West Bromwich Albion beat Everton (1 - 0)
1968-9—Manchester City beat Leicester City (1 - 0)
1969-70-Chelsea 2, Leeds United 2, after extra time at Wembley. Replay at Old Trafford - Chelsea 2, Leeds United 1, after extra time.

† A special trophy was awarded for the third consecutive win. ‡ First time final tie played in the provinces - replay at Derby. ‡‡ Replayed at Bolton. ** Replayed at Everton. *a* Replayed at Old Trafford; new trophy provided. *b* Replayed at Bramall Lane, Sheffield. †† After extra time.

Important Dates Season 1970–71

Aug 15. 1970–1 League season starts.
19. League Cup First Round.
Sept 9. League Cup Second Round.
16. European Cup Competitions.
23. Football League v Irish League.
30. European Cup Competitions.
Oct 7. Football League Cup Third Round.
14. Internationals.
21. European Cup Competitions.
28. Football League Cup Fourth Round.
Nov 4. European Cup Competitions.
11. Internationals.
18. Football League Cup Fifth Round.
21. FA Cup First Round.
25. Internationals.
Dec 2. Internationals.
9. Football League Cup semi-finals (first leg).
12. FA Cup Second Round.
16. Football League Cup semi-finals (second leg).

1971.
Jan 2. FA Cup Third Round.
13. Internationals.
23. FA Cup Fourth Round.
Feb 3. Internationals.
13. FA Cup Fifth Round.
24. Internationals.
27. League Cup Final.
Mar 6. FA Cup Sixth Round.
10. European Cup Competitions Quarter Finals.
17. Scottish League v Football League.
24. European Cup Quarter Finals.
27. FA Cup semi-finals.
April 14. European Cup Competitions semi-finals.
28. European Cup Competitions semi-finals.
May 8. FA Cup Final.
15, 22 and 29. Home International Championship.

Honours List

Club honours from The League's start in 1888 (and the preceding few seasons when subsequent League clubs were prominent in the Cup) to last season. The ratings are based on three points for League Title and FA Cup wins, two points for runners up in each competition, and one point for third in League and for the losers in FA Cup semi finals. Aston Villa have an impressive record as leaders. The table illustrates the greatness and decline of other famous clubs.

	LEAGUE			FA CUP				
Honour	Ch	2	3	W	L	SF	Total	
Points	3	2	1	3	2	1	Pts	Pos
Aston Villa	6	8	2	7	2	8	69	1
Everton	7	6	6	3	4	8	64	2
Manchester United	3	7	–	3	2	7	55	3
Sunderland	6	5	8	1	2	7	50	4
Wolves	3	5	6	4	4	2	47	5
Arsenal	7	2	3	3	3	3	46	6
Newcastle United	4	–	2	6	4	2	42	7
Sheffield Wednesday	4	1	6	3	2	8	41	8
Liverpool	7	3	1	1	2	5	40	9
Preston North End	2	6	2	2	5	3	39	10
Blackburn Rovers	2	–	3	6	2	8	39	11
West Bromwich A.	1	2	–	5	5	7	39	12
Tottenham Hotspur	2	4	5	5	–	4	38	13
Manchester City	2	2	3	4	3	2	33	14
Huddersfield Town	3	3	3	1	4	2	31	15
Sheffield United	1	2	–	4	2	4	27	16
Burnley	2	2	5	1	2	4	26	17
Derby County	–	3	3	1	3	8	18	18
Bolton Wanderers	–	–	3	4	3	5	26	19
Chelsea	1	–	3	1	2	7	21	20
Portsmouth	2	–	1	1	1	1	15	21
Nottingham Forest	–	1	–	2	–	7	15	22
Leeds United	1	3	–	–	2	2	15	22
Leicester City	–	1	1	–	4	1	12	24
Blackpool	–	1	1	1	2	–	10	25

Notts County	–	–	2	1	1	3	10	26
Birmingham	–	–	–	–	2	5	9	27
Southampton	–	–	–	–	2	5	9	28
Charlton Athletic	–	1	1	1	1	–	8	29
Cardiff City	–	1	–	1	1	1	8	30
West Ham United	–	–	–	1	1	1	6	31
Bury	–	–	–	2	–	–	6	32
Bristol City	–	1	–	–	1	1	5	33
Barnsley	–	–	–	1	1	–	5	34
Fulham	–	–	–	–	–	4	4	35
Ipswich Town	1	–	–	–	–	–	3	36
Bradford City	–	–	–	1	–	–	3	37
Oldham Athletic	–	1	–	–	–	1	3	38
Millwall	–	–	–	–	–	3	3	39
Luton Town	–	–	–	–	1	–	2	40
Swindon Town	–	–	–	–	–	2	2	41
Swansea Town	–	–	–	–	–	2	2	42
Grimsby Town	–	–	–	–	–	–	2	43

Middlesbrough, Stoke, Hull, Port Vale, Norwich, York, Reading, Crewe, Watford and Darwen have one point each for a semi-final appearance.

The League and European Football

WALTER PILKINGTON

The summit of a club's ambition was revealed when a joyful Arsenal celebrated a belated taste of glory with their first trophy success for seventeen years through winning the European Fairs Cup.

Their triumph over Anderlecht, in conjunction with the stirring performance of Cup Winners Cup victors, Manchester City, coupled with the previous successes of Manchester United, West Ham United, Newcastle, Leeds and Spurs against Europe's star teams, has made English League clubs predominant in this expanding international sphere during recent years.

The trend in our favour has also provoked sneers from critics, who could have made themselves better informed, that England would still be smugly satisfied with so-called splendid isolation if the supposed antagonism of an allegedly insular Management Committee to European football had not been overcome.

The cases cited are the 1955 and 1958 opposition to Chelsea and Manchester United participating in European competitive football as League Champions. The actual reasons were glossed over in a tirade against the presumed folly of a short-sighted, parochial approach by out-moded administrators.

Chelsea withdrew on the considered advice of the legislators that their venture would not be in the best interests of the League clubs as a whole at that time. Manchester United were asked to withdraw (the Committee had no power to compel), but objections were waived because the club had entered in good faith at the invitation of the Football Association, and had completed arrangements for home and away games with Anderlecht F.C.

The League were not, as has been contemptuously suggested, utterly out of touch with the crowd-drawing potential and jet-age possibilities of European football. They were concerned over blandishments which seemingly both challenged their authority to run their own competition as they thought best and threatened to undermine its solidarity.

Remember that the European Cup was then in the pioneering stage. The Management Committee, rightly in my view, saw an ominous red light in the linking of its development with glib forecasts of a Super-League in this country.

The secession of a coterie of powerful clubs, tempted by the lure of a possible European League, would have been a mere flight of fancy if, as now, European invitations had been confined to Champion clubs and Cup winners. They were not, and the League administrators were right in opposing selective invitations in preference to qualification solely on merit proved by performance.

Once this safeguard was assured in respect of all three major European competitions, The League worked in helpful harmony with the organisers. Forthwith they proceeded to do everything practicable to foster the success of League clubs against Europe's foremost teams, even to making the League Cup a means of entry.

Since then there has been no more talk of a Super-League.